Masculinity

A C. G. JUNG FOUNDATION BOOK

The C. G. Jung Foundation for Analytical Psychology is dedicated to helping men and women to grow in conscious awareness of the psychological realities in themselves and society, find healing and meaning in their lives and greater depth in their relationships, and to live in response to their discovered sense of purpose. It welcomes the public to attend its lectures, seminars, films, symposia, and workshops and offers a wide selection of books for sale through its bookstore. The Foundation also publishes *Quadrant*, a semiannual journal, and books on Analytical Psychology and related subjects. For information about Foundation programs or membership, please write to the C. G. Jung Foundation, 28 East 39th Street, New York, NY 10016.

MASCULINITY

Identity, Conflict, and Transformation

Warren Steinberg

Shambhala
Boston & London
1993

Shambhala Publications, Inc.
Horticultural Hall
300 Massachusetts Avenue
Boston, Massachusetts 02115

9 8 7 6 5 4 3 2 1

First Edition
Printed in the United States of America on acid-free paper ∞
Distributed in the United States by Random House, Inc.,
and in Canada by Random House of Canada Ltd

Library of Congress Cataloging-in-Publication Data

Steinberg, Warren, 1944–
    Masculinity: identity, conflict, and transformation/Warren Steinberg,—1st ed.
    p.   cm.
    "A C. G. Jung Foundation book."
    Includes bibliographical references.
    ISBN 0-87773-620-0 (alk. paper)
    1. Masculinity (Psychology)   2. Men—Psychology.   3. Sex role.
    4. Jung, C. G. (Carl Gustav), 1875–1961—Contributions in psychology
    of masculinity.   I. Title.
    BF175.5.M37S74   1993   93-2978
    155.3'32—dc20   CIP

To Moishe ben Nachman

Thank you for your contribution to my life.

Contents

Acknowledgments

I wish to thank Maurice Krasnow for reading and editing an early draft of this manuscript. I thank Julie Cashford for her dislike of bad prose. I thank Barry Steinberg for his customary generosity. Most important, I am grateful to all of them for their friendship.

Introduction

Three archetypal structures—the persona, the shadow, and the anima—are significant for the development of the masculine gender role. The need to develop and integrate the human potential symbolized by these three structures is part of the archetypal process of transformation, and their lack of development can impede that process.

The three universal structures, along with the process of transformation, provide an outline of a broad sequence of events that men need to go through in order to satisfy the teleological drive for wholeness inherent in their personalities: the need to develop into a male human being. Sociocultural, familial, and individual factors largely determine the unique way in which each male passes through the developmental sequence and whether or not he fixates at some point in the process.

Critical to the personality is the relationship between the individual and society. In adapting to society conformity is necessary. Society demands that people develop a *persona*, that is, appear and act according to certain roles. While the characteristics that define roles vary from culture to culture, that people adopt such roles is universal.

Gender roles are an aspect of the persona; they are a social construction, creating powerful expectations designed to outline acceptable behavior for each sex. Gender roles are personality characteristics of men and women developed in accordance with the psychological need to be a man or a woman and with the expectations of the particular society and culture in which a man or a woman was socialized. We all hold our own beliefs on the nature of "manhood" and "womanhood," based primarily on what we have learned or been taught to believe. What results are powerful stereotypes of masculinity and feminity, stereotypes that we accept at an early age and that influence our behavior and thoughts as men and women.

Men in our society customarily identify their gender role with the instrumental/active dimension—rational, assertive, task-oriented behavior designed to achieve a goal in the outer world. Women, on the other hand, tend to identify with the expressive/passive dimension—behavior oriented toward the expression of feeling and the management of the emotional life of the group. While there is no innate relationship between the genders and these two dimensions, there does exist a tendency, perhaps archetypal, for men to intially develop the instrumental/active dimension and women the expressive/passive dimension.

For a boy to feel adequate as a male he must develop competency in the traditional characteristics of the masculine gender role—the instrumental/active dimension. Imitation and identification with the father is how the boy seeks his masculine gender role. A nurturing, affectionate father who is perceived as powerful and valuable provides the boy with the model hs seeks, and the son wants to be like the father he loves and admires. A secure, traditional masculine gender role develops. An absent, weak, or passive father, domination of the father and the son by the mother, or domination and abuse of the son by the father, on the other hand, lead to the development of disturbed forms of the masculine gender role.

When a man does not develop competence in the traditional masculine gender role he feels inadequate. The qualities characteristic of that role remain undeveloped, associated in the unconscious with an archetypal structure that Jung called the *shadow*. Until a man has successfully developed the instrumental/active dimension—that is, made those characteristics a part of his conscious personality rather than his shadow—he will not feel adequate as a traditional man and he will not have the security to proceed further in his masculine development.

The lack of formal initiation rituals is very real in contemporary society and often results in boys never fully learning the rituals and meanings of traditional masculinity. The current men's movement tries to rectify the lack through male gatherings where rituals of male bonding under the guidance of mentors can occur. To this end, groups of men have been gathering in semiwilderness, apart from women, to engage in such activities as drumming and dancing around bonfires, hoping to free what is claimed to be a gruff, elemental "wild man" lying deep inside. Such experiences can be invaluable for men who need to emphasize the gender split with women while they develop a masculinity they can value.

While the development of a secure gender role is necessary for the male, the identification with the father and the traditional culture can also be limiting. The initiated boy becomes a man like the other men; he believes and acts like they do, not because it truly represents himself, but because that is the traditional way of men. Out of the security of the traditional, individuality must develop. After a man has successfully identified with the traditional masculine role, he is urged by the inner need for transformation to begin the process of separating his masculinity from that of his collective. Fear of deviance, feelings of betrayal and guilt, and the difficulty of withdrawing idealization from the father are all impediments that men must struggle with in separating from the father and the traditional masculine culture.

There is no evidence that men are less innately oriented toward the expressive/passive dimension than women. Due to social pressures to conform to the traditional masculine role, however, the development of the expressive/passive dimension often results in social ostracism and feelings of deviance. The expressive/passive characteristics remain unconscious; they exist as undeveloped potential represented by the *anima*, an archetypal structure that provides men with the ability to experience what is feminine in a human way.

When a man initially differentiates masculine from feminine and identifies his masculinity with the instrumental/active dimension, his anima comes to represent the traditional feminine values of the culture, that is, the expressive and passive. The teleological element of the psyche, however, causes the anima to "want" its content to be integrated by consciousness. Autonomous pressure is created within the personality to integrate the contents of the anima, that is, develop them so that they become part of the conscious personality. As long as the traditional persona is not too rigid, no significant inner conflict will attend this process. In addition, the man will realize that these characteristics are not strictly feminine but human. This realization is an important step in the teleological process of becoming a whole person.

In this book I use the expression "male human being" to refer to the whole man rather than the more common "androgyne." I find the perspective taken toward the concept of androgyny by traditional psychology inadequate. It tends to perceive androgyny as merely an addition of one set of characteristics to another, rather than a synthesis that gives rise to a new entity—an integrated human being. I use the phrase "male human being" to refer to what I consider the goal of male psychological development—wholeness.

A man who develops into a male human being does more than add traditionally feminine attributes to his masculine repertoire. He understands that they are not feminine to begin with. He realizes that the categorization of human qualities into masculine and feminine creates a false dichotomy that can only be resolved by means of an internal synthesis. All the characteristics normally considered masculine and feminine, except for a few to be discussed, are really part of his potential as a human being.

Becoming a male human being involves holding the dichotomy of masculine and feminine in consciousness until a synthesis occurs and a new integrated reaction is experienced. Maintaining consciousness of the opposites entails tension and suffering. For example, the man who is developing into a male human being suffers the tension that comes from being different from others and no longer embodying the norms of society. He sacrifices identifying with the traditional masculine gender role, which indicates his competence as a man in the eyes of society.

The benefit that a man derives from the acceptance of such conscious conflict and suffering is the ultimate transformation of the personality. That transformation results in a new image and experience of humanness, an integration that enables the man to embody more comfortably his full potential as a human being.

1 | The Basic Split

In my practice as a Jungian psychoanalyst, I have grown accustomed to women expressing dissatisfaction with their gender role. Many are no longer willing to accept the way their gender role has been defined in American society. For a number of years, especially since the advent of the feminist movement, they have been in the process of redefining themselves and what it means to be feminine. Recently, tentatively, spurred on by wives and girlfriends who no longer are willing to play the traditional feminine role that complements and makes possible the traditional masculine role, men have also begun to question what it means to be masculine in American society.

For years American society has considered "masculinity" to be the mark of the psychologically healthy male and "femininity" to be the mark of the psychologically healthy female. The roles have been clearly defined, and there has been a certain comfort in knowing one's place. About twenty years ago, however, some people, at first mostly women, began to question the status quo. They argued that our current system of differentiated gender roles had long since outlived its usefulness, and that it now served only to prevent both men and women from developing as full and complete human beings. Supporters of this position insisted that gender roles were a product of socialization—individuals learning to be masculine and feminine on the basis of what their society taught—not innate differences between men and women. They said that people should no longer be socialized to conform to outdated standards of masculinity and femininity, but that they should be encouraged to be "androgynous"—that is, rather than trained to be either masculine or feminine, people should be encouraged to develop in themselves the characteristics of both the masculine and the feminine.

What is meant by these terms: *male, female, masculine, feminine,* and *androgynous?* The terms *male* and *female* refer to sexual categories. A male is a person with a penis. While that might sound simplistic given the many other biological differences between men and women, the penis is what the doctor looks for and is the basis on which males are categorized at birth. A female is a person with a vagina. Unless something goes wrong, persons by the age of around five years will have an identity as a male or a female that matches their sexual category. How a person behaves or feels or whether that person believes certain characteristics are more appropriate for men or women has nothing to do with whether that person is male or female. The gender of the person one has sex with also plays no part in determining which category a person resides in; a homosexual is still a male and a lesbian is still a female.

Masculine and *feminine,* on the other hand, refer to gender roles—behaviors, feelings, values and attitudes—that are considered representative of each sexual category. In American society, competence, achievement, and a focus on the outside world is characteristic of the masculine gender role, as is authority, discipline, and neutral, objective, sound judgment. Femininity, on the other hand, is represented by empathy, nurturance, emotional expression, and a focus on the internal affairs of the family. Men and women who strongly embody

these characteristics are considered highly masculine or feminine, respectively.

Persons who are highly identified with their gender role are
motivated to maintain a self-image as masculine or feminine, a
goal that is accomplished not only by developing characteristics
appropriate to their gender role but also by not developing or
suppressing any behavior that might be considered undesirable
or inappropriate for their sex. Thus a masculine gender role
represents not only the endorsement of masculine attributes
but the simultaneous rejection of feminine attributes, just as a
feminine gender role represents not only the endorsement of
feminine attributes but the simultaneous rejection of masculine
attributes.

Psychological research indicates that being highly identified
with one's gender role is not desirable. For example, men and
women who are more gender typed have been found to run a
greater risk of divorce and tend to display lower overall intelligence, lower spatial ability, and lower creativity. Women who
are strongly identified with traditional standards of femininity
have consistently been shown to have high levels of anxiety,
low self-esteem, and low social acceptance. While men who are
highly identified with traditional masculine values are better ad-
justed psychologically during adolescence, as adults they also
experience high anxiety, high neuroticism, and low self-accept-
ance.[1]

In addition to its psychological costs, identifying strongly
with masculinity or femininity is deleterious to physical health.
This is especially true for men. Because of their image of self-
sufficiency, outer orientation, and strength, men are reluctant
to seek professional help, especially if the difficulties are psychological in nature.[2] Perhaps that is why men are twice as
likely to die of heart attacks than are women, why the suicide

rate for men is over two and a half times that of women, and why alcoholism kills men more frequently than women. In addition, men are less likely than women to perform routine preventive health behaviors such as immunizations, teeth brushing, and getting adequate sleep.

For many people, adhering to traditional gender roles produces unnecessary and even dysfunctional avoidance patterns. In one study, females who valued traditional feminine attitudes actively avoided nailing two boards together and gender-typed males refused to wind a package of yarn into a ball, just because those activities happen to be stereotyped as more appropriate for the other gender. When actually required to perform such activities, both men and women reported discomfort and even some temporary loss of self-esteem.[3]

There is clear evidence that for adults overidentification with masculine and feminine roles is not the healthiest physical or psychological adaptation. Why do we continue to limit human potential in this way?

Those who insist on the significance of the biological differences between men and women see gender differences as purely biological factors. Such advocates of the traditionalist view of gender believe that men innately possess "masculine" characteristics such as strength, aggression, rationality, independence, and task orientation. Women, on the other hand, innately possess "feminine" characteristics such as gentleness, passivity, intuitiveness, dependence, and an orientation to relationship.

The polarization of gender characteristics based on innate, biological differences has attributed greater human differences to the sexes than really exist. A few apparent biological or socialized sex differences have been generalized incorrectly to many unrelated skills, attitudes, and behaviors of males and females. For instance, because women lactate and have, at least before the advent of infant formula, been forced by biological necessity to nurture, it has been generalized that women are nurturant and men are not. From this initial generalization comes the further generalization that because men are not innately nuturant they are also deficient in interpersonal relatedness. But to nurture is not necessarily to be nurturant, and there are many different ways for people to be related other than to feed each other. Because of these types of simplistic and unwarranted generalizations, people have been encouraged to identify with the stereotyped communication styles and behavior patterns that traditionally represent their gender. As a result, men and women have usually learned only a portion of the skills, feelings, values, and behaviors necessary to cope effectively and fully with life.

Androgyny represents the ability to experience the attributes normally considered "masculine" and "feminine" without regard for their association to a sexual category. Recent research shows that an androgynous view of oneself is accompanied by greater maturity in one's moral judgments, a higher level of self-esteem, and greater flexibility in adapting to diverse situations.[4] Because an androgynous self-definition excludes neither masculinity nor femininity, one is better able to remain sensitive to the changing constraints of a situation and engage in whatever behavior seems most effective at the moment, regardless of its stereotype as appropriate for one sex or the other. Androgynous individuals can do things typically associated with the opposite gender with little reluctance or discomfort. For instance, they can display both "masculine" independence when under pressure to conform as well as "feminine" nurturance when given the opportunity to interact in an expressive way.

Yet a man may do more than merely add traditionally feminine attributes to his masculine repertoire—that is, become what traditional psychology labels an "androgyne." Instead, he may synthesize both sets of characteristics in order to become more fully human—to become what, in the case of a man, I prefer to call a "male human being." To illustrate the distinction: An androgynous person would be able to move from typically "masculine" to typically "feminine" attributes as the situation demanded; the androgynous male, for instance, could fire an employee without a second thought and then come home and be sensitive and loving toward his wife and children. The male human being, on the other hand, synthesizes the traditional masculine and feminine qualities so that when he fires the employee he feels something about the effect he is having on a fellow human being. He is aware of the necessity of the decision, acts with compassion and sensitivity, and also suffers the guilt that accrues to the person who consciously experiences the damage caused to another.

Besides the tension generated by deviating from the traditional masculine gender role, the man who is becoming a male human being also suffers the tension that comes from holding conflicting values in consciousness. It would have been easier for the employer to either be "masculine" and fire the person without feeling, or to be "feminine" and keep the person on the payroll out of compassion. Synthesizing the two positions entails consciousness of the morality of acting out a decision that is correct in terms of external obligations but wrong in terms of feeling obligations to a fellow human being. Guilt is the suffering that results. Accepting such conscious conflict and suffering is a necessary part of the ultimate transformation of the personality.

It seems evident that, for both men and women, living as whole human beings is healthier than identification with one-sided maculine and feminine roles. Why do we then continue to split reality into opposites and limit human potential? If the role differences between men and women are not fundamentally based on biological differences, why do we not raise children to be whole human beings, teaching them the full range of attributes, feelings, attitudes, and adaptations of being human regardless of whether they are traditionally associated to the male or female gender?

Because, unfortunately, the human psyche does not work that way.

THE DEVELOPMENT OF CONSCIOUSNESS AND THE BASIC SPLIT

Gender identity is one's personal and private experience of gender: the concept of self as either male or female. "I am a male" is a statement about gender identity.

The gender in which a child is reared in infancy establishes in the child a psychological gender identity that is practically irreversible. While there is no conclusive evidence about the processes involved in the formation of a stable gender identity, it is generally agreed that it is complete for most children between the ages of three to five. Children at this age can make firm statements about their gender, and they cannot be reassigned to another gender without incurring severe psychological disturbance. Once the child knows to which gender category he or she belongs, psychological processes act to bring about further differentiation of psychological traits and behaviors appropriate to the child's gender. The child begins to acquire the complement of temperamental and behavioral attributes that society has defined as appropriate to his or her gender.

A gender role is a constellation of qualities a person understands to characterize males and females in his or her culture.

It provides a script for playing the roles of male and female in a society. Both men and women must be aware of male and female role scripts to judge the appropriateness of others' behavior and to respond properly to the lead of the other.

Several competing theories attempt to account for gender identity and gender role acquisition. Social-learning theory states that gender identity results from learning gender-related behaviors. Psychoanalytic theory, on the other hand, states that gender identity results from identification with the same-sex parent; a boy becomes masculine because he has identified with his father. In contrast, cognitive theory hypothesizes that gender identity precedes and determines learning and identification.

One person who studied the development of cognition in children concluded that children go through a series of maturational stages that includes structuring the world by categorizing it into opposites: hot-cold, wet-dry, good tasting–bad tasting.[5] Male-female is one such set of opposites, and every person must be in one category or the other. So the child first establishes its gender as male or female, then proceeds to acquire and value those attributes, behaviors, and attitudes associated with his or her gender. Gender identity precedes and determines gender role. The boy, for instance, seeks to acquire attributes that will help him develop and confirm the gender category to which he has realized he belongs. That is the reason why the boy comes to identify with his father; he realizes that he and his father belong to the same category of "we males," and by becoming like the father the boy can develop his own masculinity. The attributes that the boy will come to value are those embodied by the father and significant other males in his society: competence, strength, power, and instrumental achievement.

In addition, according to another authority, in the course of ego development children go through a normal stage of conformity during which rules are partially internalized and obeyed just because they are the rules.[6] Characteristic of this stage, which reaches its peak in adolescence, is the tendency to describe oneself in socially desirable terms and to experience shame for transgression of that which is socially acceptable.

This stage of conformity coincides with the stage at which gender roles are acquired. Children become obsessed with rules and external appearances and become aggravated when they perceive deviations from rules. During this stage, boys and girls are socialized differently, and they develop a set of gender role stereotypes conforming to the cultural definitions. Little boys are taught to control the expression of feelings and affects, while assertion and extention of self are abetted. Little girls are taught to control aggression, including assertion and extension, while being encouraged to regard the inner, familial world as the proper sphere of their interest. Communion is emphasized in the development of girls but is explicitly discouraged in boys.

Thus, at the cognitive stage when male and female become distinct categories experienced as opposites, the child seeks to conform to one or the other. To abet the need to conform, the child naturally identifies with the more similar parent; family and society further the identification with gender roles through socialization pressures that encourage and discourage particular behaviors in boys and girls.

That children hold more rigid gender stereotypes than adults may account for some of the difficulty many liberated parents and teachers have in trying to raise children androgynously. These adults have worked unstintingly to provide an environment free of gender biases for their children by limiting the child's exposure to stereotypical gender models. The parents provide dolls for boys and encourage the development of the relational side of their personalities; girls are encouraged to be assertive and may even be given guns to play "war" with. Yet the parents are confounded when their young children insist on the truth of old stereotypes.

I remember a personal experience observing my own son and daughter that illustrates the adherence children have to gender stereotypes. My daughter, who was then five years old, was the "mommy" in the game she and my son, then three years old, were playing. She wanted to drive their toy car to the fantasy picnic they were going on with their toy children. My son, the "daddy," declared heatedly that she could not because "only daddies do that." My daughter promptly said: "Okay, I'll be the daddy now." She became daddy and "drove" the car around the living room. In order to maintain consonance between gender and stereotypical activity, my daughter had switched genders in order to perform the activity reserved for the masculine gender.

Recognizing phases of development will help parents respond appropriately to the child's need to engage only in traditional gender-appropriate activities, or to exclude the other sex from them. During such a phase, children may reject nontraditional patterns if presented to them. The conformist stage of development normally peaks in early adolescence, when traditional masculine-feminine gender role patterns are at their height.

The traditionalist view of masculinity and femininity maintains .that the roles that men and women play are a natural outgrowth of innate differences between the sexes, and traditionalists argue for a rigid adherence to gender roles. For them, the roles developed during the conformist stage become the final ones. Unfortunately, the traditionalist's model of mature male and female gender roles remains identified with the gender role conceptions of eleventh-grade boys and girls. The conformist view does not take into account later life experiences that loosen one's conception of oneself as a man or a woman. The real risk for gender role development, thus, is not that persons may fail to reach the conformist stage, but that they may never leave it.

After the conformist stage, for those who continue their development, come the conscientious, autonomous, and integrated levels of development, which are stages one may experience in adolescence and adulthood.

During the conscientious stage one begins a self-conscious process of evaluating oneself relative to one's own internalized values and the prevailing expectations of the culture. In terms of gender development, the individual begins to compare and balance the collective definitions of masculine and feminine with his or her own nature.

During the autonomous stage of development there develops a greater tolerance of those who choose other solutions to life's conflicts. Men no longer have to conform to rigid traditionalist stereotypes of masculinity; women can experiment with the adoption of traditionally male characteristics. In contrast to the condemnation characteristic of the conformist stage, one recognizes the autonomy of the individual and tolerates deviance from collective norms.

Finally, for the fortunate, the integrated level of development occurs. One moves beyond coping with conflict to the reconciliation of conflicting demands, beyond mere toleration to the full appreciation of individual differences, beyond role differentiation to the achievement of a sense of integrated wholeness. For men who reach this stage—the integration of masculinity and femininity—self-assertion, self-interest, and self-extensions become tempered by considerations of mutuality and interdependence.[7] For women, on the other hand, the functioning of the group, the submersion of self, and the importance of consensus are amended to include self-assertion and self-expression, aspects that are essential for personal integration and self-actualization.

THE JUNGIAN MODEL

We have discussed how cognitive theory suggests that the human psyche has an inherent propensity to create mental categories that divide the experience of the world into opposites. The idea of splitting psychological reality into opposites is essential for the understanding of Jungian psychology. According to Jung, this splitting into opposites occurs on two levels. First, there is a primary splitting of the totality of the human psyche into conscious and unconscious. Second, there is the working of consciousness, which discriminates contents into opposites through the four functions—thinking, feeling, sensation, and intuition. On both levels of splitting, masculinity and femininity are affected.

According to Jung, the primary splitting of the psyche into conscious and unconscious not only is the basis for the experience of external reality being organized psychologically into oppositional categories, but may actually be the cause of the division. The psyche projects its own condition onto the external world in symbolic form, and the external reality is then determined by the symbols.

The psyche, according to Jung, symbolizes the opposites of conscious and unconscious by means of masculine and feminine images. The split of the human psyche into conscious and unconscious is then projected onto external reality through masculine and feminine images, which in turn determine and organize reality in terms of these two categories.

Because of the projection of the masculine and feminine as symbols of conscious and unconscious, a person experiences not only external conditions but also certain psychological attributes as dichotomous and antithetical. For example, the ego, rationality, and spirituality are identified with masculinity and consciousness. They are opposed by the feminine condition of unconsciousness, whose "bodily appetites and . . . heart's affections" disturb the rationality of the mind.[8] The psychological attributes are often, owing to the tendency to concretize symbols, then mistakenly understood as actually belonging to different genders in reality, not just symbolically. As a consequence, people believe that certain psychological functions such as thinking and feeling are inherently more characteristic of either the masculine or feminine gender, respectively.

The second split is characteristic of the working of consciousness itself. Jung says that consciousness and understanding arise from discrimination followed by synthesis. The four orienting functions of consciousness discriminate a psychic content into four aspects. The four functions are two pairs of opposites: thinking and feeling oppose each other, as do sensation and intuition. Consciousness perceives and assimilates each of the parts in turn, creating through synthesis the whole that had been sundered.

Jung, of course, developed the idea of innate structures that organize information into categories.[9] These he called the *archetypes*. Since much of this book involves a more detailed discussion of the archetypes in relationship to masculine gender development, I will just say a few words about archetypes in general for those to whom the concept is new.

Jung's formulation of the concept of the archetype changed over the years. Initially he used terms like *archetypal image*, which implied that what was inherited was a specific image. In his later writings Jung opted to describe archetype as *pattern*. By this he meant that the archetypes did not have a fixed content, that only their form was inherent. He said, "The archetype in itself is empty and purely formal . . . a possibility of representation which is given *a priori*. The representations themselves are not inherited, only the forms, and in that respect they correspond in every way to the instincts, which are also determined in form only."[10]

Despite Jung's clarifications, much confusion revolves around the term *archetype*. Too often an archetype is confused with a cultural stereotype, for example. To clarify, we could understand an archetype to be composed of three elements: an instinctive dynamism, a psychic structure, and the culturally determined images that fill out the structure.

First, on a biological level, an archetype is an instinctive pattern of behavior, similar to the instinctive behavior of nonhuman species. Jung said, "Of course this term is not meant to denote an inherited idea, but rather an inherited mode of psychic functioning, corresponding to the inborn way in which the chick emerges from the egg, the bird builds its nest, a certain kind of wasp stings the motor ganglion of the caterpillar, and eels find their way to the Bermudas. In other words, it is a 'pattern of behavior.' "[11]

Second, in contrast to theorists who assumed the newborn was a tabula rasa with no innate psychological structures to organize information, Jung assumed the existence of psychic structures that organize experience. For example, the contrasexual archetypes, the anima and animus, predispose us to organize relevant information about males and females of the human species in a particularly human way. These archetypes are the initial core around which gender categories are built, and they even determine the dichotomizing of existence into opposites of masculine and feminine.

Third, there are the cultural facts that fill out the structure. The latter are a personal acquisition and are all we really know about the archetype. A mistake that is so often made is to confuse the particular cultural facts with the archetype. Jung said, "The unconscious supplies as it were the archetypal form, which in itself is empty and irrepresentable. Consciousness immediately fills it with related or similar representational material so that it can be perceived. For this reason archetypal ideas are locally, temporally, and individually conditioned."[12]

In our culture, for example, women are supposed to be passive, dependent, intuitive, and feeling oriented; men are supposed to be aggressive and analytical. From the cultural facts of our typical patriarchal Western society we derive a masculine and a feminine principle, which are then projected onto their respective archetypes. All the archetypes give us, however, is the ability to experience men and women in a human way. The *nature* of the experience is cultural. For example, the anima permits us to experience women as passive and nurturant, but it does not require us to do that. The contrasexual archetypes would also permit us to experience other patterns if our culture allowed it. In the Tchambuli culture, for example, women are aggressive and independent and men are relatively passive and dependent.[13]

While Jung's idea of the fundamental split into opposites and the idea of innate organizing categories are important for the development of gender roles, the most important of his contributions, in my opinion, is his proposition that there exists an inherent tendency, a teleological drive, to move from conforming to oppositional categories toward a synthesis of masculine and feminine.

In contrast to a cause-and-effect perspective that assumes that natural processes can be explained by preceding events, a teleological position assumes that life has purpose. Events develop the way they do because they are heading in a certain direction, toward a goal that can be seen in them.

For Jung, dividing the personality into such structures as ego, persona, shadow, and anima was not an adequate description of the psyche. The idea of transformation was also necessary. There is a developmental urge inherent in the psyche, which Jung called the *individuation process*—a drive to integrate the unconscious, unite the opposites, and achieve wholeness.

"There is no doubt the goal of the philosophical alchemist was higher self-development . . . what I would call individuation. . . . Nor is he aware that by knocking on the door of the unknown he is obeying the law of the inner, future man, and that he is disobedient to this law whenever he seeks to secure a permanent advantage or possession from his work. Not his ego, that fragment of a personality, is meant; it is rather that a wholeness, of which he is a part, wants to be transformed from a latent state of unconsciousness into an approximate consciousness of itself."[14]

According to Jung, then, the splitting of psychological reality into conflicting opposites is not a goal in itself. It is only a means to an end—the conscious experience of wholeness. In order to bring about subsequent union there must first be separation, "for only separated things can unite."[15] The split state causes suffering and tension due to the pressures exerted by the drive toward wholeness. The alleviation of those pressures requires further psychological development, the integration by consciousness of the split-off parts of the personality. The dissociation of personality is thus a necessary step in a teleological process, the first stage of what Jung called the *unio mentalis*.

An important question for Jung was how people could extricate themselves from the opposites and achieve wholeness. Often people attempt to solve the conflict by identifying with one side and renouncing the other; for example, by becoming a traditional man or a traditional woman. That attempt at ending the inner struggle and achieving wholeness inevitably fails. In fifty years of writing on the subject of the opposites Jung concluded that the resolution of a conflict does not come from the acceptance of one side and repression of the other. The way to deal with the conflict of opposites is by holding both sides of the conflict in consciousness until out of the tension of opposites a resolving third arises, which unites the opposing tendencies. In terms of gender, this means that while it is necessary to first develop as a man or a woman, at some point in our development the tension of the opposite gender has to be held in consciousness until a resolving experience leads us toward the closest approximation of wholeness of which we are capable.

The Archetypal Dimensions

Jung's position is that the human psyche's split into conscious and unconscious results in a division in the experience and organization of external reality. Psychological observation has indicated that there are two broad symbolic dimensions into which the psyche consistently divides reality. Jung called these dimensions masculine and feminine. Sigmund Freud called them active and passive. Talcott Parsons, a sociologist, labeled them instrumental and expressive. The ancient Chinese called then yang and yin. Despite the different labels, the characteristics associated with these dimensions are generally consistent. For the sake of expression, I will refer to the dimensions as instrumental/active and expressive/passive.

The instrumental/active dimension is oriented toward the achievement of goals through the manipulation of the object world. It is exemplified by activities that are affectively neutral, achievement oriented, rational, and nonemotional. Initiative, decisiveness, and assertive activity are characteristic of the instrumental/active dimension, as is the urge to master and the repression of thought, feeling, and impulse. In group situations, individuals manifesting this dimension tend to take charge, give suggestions and opinions, differentiate parts of the problem to be solved, gather information, and concentrate activity in the task area.

The expressive/passive dimension is oriented toward fostering the harmony of the group through the expression and management of feelings and emotions. Activities such as laughing, playing, and expressing affection and warmth are characteristic of the expressive/passive dimension, as is the tendency to yield to more aggressive, task-oriented individuals. In group situations, individuals manifesting this dimension tend to give positive and negative emotional responses directly to other members of the group, help to release tension, and function as mediators.

It is a common observation and a psychological fact that men traditionally manifest the instrumental/active dimension and females the expressive/passive dimension. The basis for this relationship between gender and dimension is a matter of controversy. Do the external norms result from the projection of an internal archetypal pattern or biological predisposition? Do the traditional norms that males and females manifest in their gender roles really indicate innate underlying masculine and feminine principles? Or is the manifest relationship between the masculine and feminine genders and the instrumental/active and expressive/passive dimensions actually a function of socialization processes?[16]

In my opinion, the instrumental/active dimension is not reflective of a masculine principle that determines the masculine gender role, nor does the expressive/passive dimension determine femininity. What is archetypal, I would suggest, is the tendency for the psyche to split reality into opposing dimensions, as well as the dimensions themselves. That is, there is an archetypal tendency to organize reality into oppositional categories whose characteristics coincide with the instrumental/active and expressive/passive dimensions. These dimensions are historically and culturally consistent. The identification of these dimensions with the masculine and feminine genders, however, is largely determined by the tendency to concretize symbols and the socialization processes that occur in family and society.[17]

Does this mean there are no differences between men and women, merely culturally defined gender roles? I do not believe that to be the case either. While the energies that manifest in the various human behaviors, attitudes, and abilities of men and women are universal, I would suggest that the experiential quality of the behaviors, aptitudes, and attitudes that constitute the instrumental/active and expressive/passive dimensions differ, owing to the biological and anatomical differences between men and women. What differ are the psychological experiences males and females have when they engage in these human activities.

For instance, I do not believe that men will ever understand the experience of being penetrated in the same way as will a woman. A sexually active woman is used to physical penetration and derives much of her pleasure from relaxing into the feeling, whereas a man's pleasure comes from physically penetrating. Such anatomical distinctions give to the experience of penetration a qualitative difference, which lies in the instrumental/active dimension.

The hormonal differences between males and females also lead to a difference in psychological experience. I do not believe that a man's inner experience of nurturing can be identical with that of a woman, owing to the hormones that underlay lactation and a woman's ability to breast-feed an infant. In like manner, the quantity of androgen in which the male fetal brain is bathed will give him a qualitatively (not quantitatively) different experience of aggression from what a woman experiences—a point discussed further in the next chapter of this book.

While the psychological experience may differ, however, the ability to be aggressive, penetrated, related, nurturant, independent, passive, and autonomous are human and common to males and females. Difference in experience does not necessarily result in difference in ability. Because the males of the species, with their greater mobility and physical strength, became the hunters and defenders of the group does not make men inherently more aggressive than females. Lactation and a biological disposition to nurture does not make females more nurturant than men. To nurture and to be nurturant are not synonymous. The anatomical penis does not make males more penetrative. Vaginas equip women to be physically penetrated, not more receptive psychologically. Even less valid are the broader generalizations from greater musculature and penises to assertion and instrumentality, or from nurture and vaginas to relatedness, communicativeness, and expressivity. These are simplistic overgeneralizations.

What the original evolutionary assignation of instrumental/ active and expressive/passive functions may determine is the timing in which the archetypal dimensions are encountered in contemporary life. That is, it could be speculated that, because of the evolutionary history of the human species, an archetypal difference between males and females exists in the sequence in which the instrumental/active and expressive/passive dimensions are integrated. Such a sequential difference might account for the tendency of the instrumental/active and expressive/ passive norms to be so consistently associated with the masculine and feminine gender roles, respectively.

It is an error, however, to think that because something is encountered first in a sequence, it is more representative of the nature of the person who encounters it. That males first encounter and develop the instrumental/active dimension does not make the characteristics of that dimension more representative of masculinity than the qualities they encounter later in their development. Otherwise, one would have to conclude that it is more human to crawl than to stand up and walk, since the human infant first encounters crawling. If the child were encouraged to believe that its true nature was represented by crawling it would have little impetus to continue its developmental sequence to upright mobility. Similarly, the problem for men is that they are encouraged by their sociocultural environment to identify with the instrumental/active dimension and not continue toward their true goal—wholeness, becoming a male human being.

OUT OF THE STATE OF original wholeness, as a result of the normal processes of development, the male child splits psychological reality into oppositional categories, one of which is masculine-feminine. The boy realizes that he is assigned to one of the categories and, again out of the normal processes of development, seeks to develop himself in terms of that category; that is, he strives to develop his masculine gender role. Becoming a "traditional" male through the integration of the gender characteristics encouraged by his society does not satisfy the need for wholeness, however. The inherent demand for transformation necessitates further development, development that can be satisfied only by movement toward becoming a male human being. This movement involves recognizing, developing, and integrating into one's personality all of the characteristics that have been left undeveloped because they have been associated with the feminine gender role.

Men in our society customarily identify their gender role with the instrumental/active dimension—rational, assertive, task-oriented behavior designed to achieve a goal in the outer world. Women, on the other hand, tend to identify with the expressive/passive dimension. While there is no innate relationship between the genders and the instrumental/active and expressive/passive dimensions, the tendency to split reality into oppositional dimensions, like the dimensions themselves, has an archetypal basis. Furthermore, the dimensions may be experienced in an archetypal sequence that differs for men and women.

Failure to continue development is, according to Jung, one of the primary causes of neurotic conflict. In terms of gender, failure to develop out of the conformist phase of identity with oppositional categories will create conflict as surely as will failure to identify adequately with the appropriate gender category during the conformist phase of development. Only wholeness will satisfy the teleological urge for development inherent in the psyche. For men, conforming to the instrumental/active dimension and failure to develop the expressive/passive side of their nature is the primary impediment toward wholeness—toward becoming a male human being.

The necessity for men to develop wholeness, as well as some of the typical conflicts that arise when that development is inhibited, is the primary emphasis of this book. In the service of such understanding I will sketch a broad outline of a Jungian theory of gender development, with masculinity used as a model.

2 | Male-Male Competition
Anatomy of an Archetype

Before we can discuss the developmental sequence by which a boy assumes the masculine gender role and a man may transcend that role to become a male human being, another question must first be addressed: do universal patterns of behavior and feeling exist that are uniquely and innately masculine? That is, are there forces inherent to the psyche that account for the development of the characteristics traditional to the masculine gender role? Are the traditional norms of the masculine gender role a manifestation of an underlying "masculine principle"?

Some authors answer this question by attributing all gender characteristics to socialization processes. While they acknowledge that certain innate physiologic and anatomic differences distinguish men from women, they insist that all psychological and behavioral differences in the masculine and feminine gender roles are societally and culturally determined.[1] These writers disregard, not only the effects of instincts on patterns of gender behavior, but also how the evolutionary eons have etched patterns of experience, feeling, and behavior into human beings.

In contrast, other writers on the subject of gender roles suggest many innate characteristics for males and females. Jung, for instance, suggested distinct cognitive styles as masculine and feminine—Logos as characterizing the consciousness of men and Eros that of females. Robert Bly discusses different masculine and feminine patterns of energy symbolized by various mythological figures. Jean Bolen describes different patterns of masculinity symbolized by the Greek gods.[2]

I find these assignments of masculine and feminine patterns simplistic, indicating either the cultural norms of the time or the projection of such norms onto the interpretation of mythology. Is there any evidence other than cultural norms that male consciousness is characterized more by Logos than by Eros? Are there no mythologies that indicate that males are receptive and females erect and instigating? Myths do not state the absolute nature of what is masculine or feminine. They indicate archetypal potentials for being fully human and how cultures have traditionally parceled out those potentials on the basis of gender.

We need to be careful in assuming inherent biological or archetypal differences between masculine and feminine gender roles. Serious difficulties hamper us in making such determinations. On the one hand, there is the danger of assuming that all behaviors characteristic of the masculine and feminine gender roles are socially conditioned. People striving to change themselves into what they were never meant to be, on the basis of current social thinking, may too easily disregard the drives and needs inherent to men and women. On the other hand, the assumption of innate patterns runs the danger of reinforcing ancient cultural prejudices that prevent people from becoming fully human.

My position is that most, but not all, patterns of behavior and feeling attributed to men and women are socially conditioned, not innate. To discover what is truly particular to men and women we must first divest ourselves of the stereotypes inculcated by society. We then discover a remarkable potential to be truly and fully human, a condition for men that I call being a male human being.

This is not to say that there are no innate patterns of masculine and feminine behavior or experience, only that one has to avoid facile and superficial conclusions. Sociological findings, biology, comparison of species, and mythology are all necessary to lend support to purported archetypal patterns. In the previous chapter I suggested that the sequence in which the instrumental/active and expressive/passive dimensions are developed and integrated in men and women is archetypally based. In this chapter, I discuss an aspect of aggression—male-male competition for dominance—where evidence suggests that an archetypal pattern of behavior and experience exist. (The topic of male domination of females is discussed more fully in chapter 6. The evidence indicates that male domination of females is socially conditioned, not archetypally based.)

MALE-MALE COMPETITION FOR DOMINANCE

No evidence supports the common social stereotype that men are inherently more aggressive than women.[3] What differs for men and women is rather the inner experience of aggression and the situations that elicit the aggressive response. Some events arouse aggression more quickly in men, while other events arouse aggression more quickly in women. John Money's research, for example, suggests that men respond more quickly with aggression around issues of territoriality and hierarchical struggle. Women, on the other hand, respond more quickly with aggression when their young are threatened.[4] A promising area, then, in which to seek archetypal patterns is not the instinct per se, but rather the particular situations that elicit the aggressive reaction. One area where research indicates that an inherent universal pattern may exist is male-male competition for dominance, a characteristic of the masculine gender role and a derivative of the instrumental/active dimension: control of the environment to achieve a goal.

Jung suggested that we may at times project archetypal images which then organize our perceptions of that reality.[5] This seems be the case with male-male competition for dominance. We project the underlying archetypal pattern onto our culture and thereby cause the culture to socialize males to conform to the pattern. The archetypal pattern determines the development of the conventional masculine gender role by encouraging individual males to find men who are dominant to other men as models to emulate.

Male-male competition for dominance has roots beyond human socialization processes, though the latter may form its expression. It is evident among males of many species and, as a matter of fact, the struggle to prevail over competing males often seems to dwarf all other tasks. Rams butting heads during mating season, chimpanzees mounting weaker members of the troop to show their dominant position in the hierarchy, human males saying they "have been screwed" when another male has taken advantage of them are all examples of this pattern.

Male-male competition for dominance has a physiological substrate. Biologists studying the African cichlid fish have discovered in the hypothalamus of aggressive males brain cells that allow the fish to mate which are six to eight times larger than the equivalent cells in mild-mannered males with no social clout. What is more, the dimensions of those cells are extremely plastic. Should the domineering male be confronted by a larger male able to bully it, the neurons of the defeated fish will rapidly shrink. And after the hypothalmic cells have shrunk, the male's testes follow suit, eventually robbing the fish of its desire and ability to breed.[6]

If one were to attribute human psychological processes to the defeated fish whose testes have shrunk and desire to breed have diminished, we might imagine that the fish feels castrated and humiliated; that is, the fish experiences a decrement in its masculine gender role.

If a dominant male disappears, all the meek males in the neighborhood rush over, seeking to fill the vacancy, and a series of violent battles commences. Eventually, a winner emerges and promptly begins flaunting his success through telltale displays of dominance and territoriality. At that point a welter of physical changes begins. The male grows bigger and gains a bright coat; its gonads swell and it starts making sperm.

If we were to continue our anthropomorphic fantasy about the fish's psychological life, we could imagine that the fish feels phallic and potent. He experiences an enhancement of his masculine gender role and is filled with masculine pride.

Taking the fish back to the laboratory, the researchers found that the behavioral changes occur first, and that they in turn spur dramatic growth in brain cells responsible for producing a compound called gonadotropin-releasing hormone. That substance tweaks the pituitary gland to produce hormones that in turn stimulate the fish's testes and switch on sperm production. Conversely, in experiments where a dominant male is stripped of its preeminence by the introduction of a bigger, nastier male, the chastened fish stops making dominant displays and slinks off, and the brain changes follow. Within days, its bright colors have disappeared and its testicles have withered.

In a similar vein, moving up the evolutionary scale, monkeys and baboons on the lower rungs of the hierarchical ladder seem to be inhibited and inactive sexually. This is probably because they are constantly subject to the threatening watchfulness of the head of the troop. In addition, the subordinate bachelors have penises of a smaller size and a paler color than those at the top. It appears that it is the subordination that effects the development of the genitals, not the other way round.

These fish and monkey examples are evidence of how social interactions can sculpt the structure of the brain and the development of the physiological organs and how the altered brain and physiology, in turn, influence behavior. It may also have relevance for such creatures as human beings. Because the brain molecules of the cichlid fish under study are highly conserved across the evolutionary spectrum, it can be conjectured that the architecture of the human brain may also be affected by a person's behavior. Similarly, monkeys and baboons are not so distant on the evolutionary scale that extrapolations to human beings cannot be considered. Is it not possible for patterns of behavior lived for eons by the evolutionary ancestors of the human species to have been etched into the nervous system of human beings and now to function autonomously?

While some might argue that the jump from cichlid fish and monkeys to humans is too great, the idea that it is not just structure or hormones that influence behavior but behavior and the environment that influence hormones, structure, and consequent psychological experience can be validated, especially for the issue of male-male competition for dominance.

Fluctuations in testosterone levels in the 20 to 30 percent range have been found to reflect competitive triumphs and defeats. Studies suggest that the hormone may be sensitive to the ups and downs of competition. In one study the testosterone levels of the members of a tennis team were monitored before and after six meets. Results showed that testosterone levels rose in those who won. In the same vein, other studies showed a rise in testosterone levels in the hours after men were awarded their M.D. degrees. And, conversely, it was found that testosterone levels fell in men going through harassment during the first few weeks of officers' candidate school.[7]

How well the players felt they performed was also strongly related to the hormone levels: the higher the level of testosterone, the better the player evaluated his own performance. That is, there is a relationship between testosterone level and the inner psychological experience of optimism, potency, and self-esteem.

Thus a man who says he feels like a "big dick" after a victory over a rival may be describing the psychological experience (phallic potency) that follows a physiological event (increased levels of testosterone) which in turn has been stimulated by a social behavior (competitive victory). Similarly, when a man describes himself as feeling "castrated" after domination by another man, that feeling of castration, as if the man has no penis or it has shrunk in size, may be a valid psychological experience that is derivative of a physiological substrate. The quantity of testosterone in his blood, and perhaps even the cells in his brain that regulate the size of his penis, diminish in quantity and size and his inner experience follows accordingly.

In this sense it could be speculated that an archetypal pattern exists in regard to male-male competition for dominance. The pattern would be that males are universally programmed to respond to competitive situations with other males for dominance. One aspect of this archetypal pattern would be the production of fantasies and consequent emotions that precede and follow on competitive situations with other males. Triumph produces one kind of fantasy and emotion, defeat another. Males who win such competitions get not only the external spoils, such as the females, but also the internal experience of male potency. In humans, this internal experience consists of pride, virility, self-confidence, and power. Males who lose suffer the internal pain of "castration," loss of virility, loss of self-confidence, loss of a felt sense of masculine potency.

The archetypal pattern of male-male competition for dominance may underlie situations as diverse as the difficulties males often have in therapy with male therapists and the father-son competition that Freud described during the Oedipal phase of development.

Freud attributed the Oedipal conflict to competitive feelings the son has toward his father for the boy's mother, which as a consequence lead the boy, out of fear of castration, to identify with the father and assume a masculine role. Evidence presented elsewhere in this book disputes the idea that fear of aggression is the basis for masculine gender role development and indicates the development of the masculine gender role is an archetypal dynamic, not a neurotic defense.

The father-son competition that Freud observed does exist, however, even if he did not properly understand its source and consequence. The father-son competition during the Freudian Oedipal stage is a universal phenomenon, but it is a specific manifestation of the underlying archetypal pattern of males competing for dominance, not for the female in the house. It is this archetypal dynamic that best accounts for boys' having more aggressive fantasies toward their fathers than do girls and for boys' having them more toward their fathers than toward their mothers. These aggressive fantasies begin when boys are about three years of age, the same time as when the categories of masculine and feminine are differentiated and the boy becomes aware that he and his father are of the same gender. At the same time that the boy looks to idealize and model himself after his father, competitive and aggressive fantasies make themselves known. One way to understand these seemingly contradictory impulses is to hypothesize an opposition between a male need to compete with other males for dominance (the instrumental/active dimension) and a male need to submit to other males for transformation (the expressive/passive dimension), two archetypal forces that provide a tension out of which growth ensues. (The need men have to submit to other men, and the role submission plays in the process of male transformation, will be discussed more fully in the last chapter of this book.)

One man began therapy with the hope that I could help him with his anxieties about masculinity. He developed an early idealization evidenced by his attempts to dress like me and get my opinion on the best way to handle various situations typical for the insecure male, such as how to impress women and to perform better sexually. At the same time, he tried to compete with me for dominance in many ways, insisting that I open a window when it was closed or close it if it were open, dim a light or put on the air conditioner, whichever was opposite to how it was when he entered the room. If I made an observation about his psychology or behavior he became argumentative, challenging the validity of even the most simple and obvious interventions.

Since this young man had an aggressive, dominating, and critical father, I at first assumed that his competitive behavior in therapy was a reaction to a projection of his father onto my person; that is, he experienced my observations as a repetition of his father's criticisms. By disagreeing with me whenever possible and taking control of my office environment he could show me that he was in control and that I could not dominate him.

A dream that the patient reported approximately three

months after beginning therapy indicated that something more universal might underlie his competitive behavior with me and perhaps even that of the competition between the patient and his father:

> My father and I are compelled by some force internal to both of us to fight and then compare the size of our penises. My father won the fight and when we compared penises my father's was larger. That was confusing because I knew that my own penis had been larger before the fight. Now that my father had won I expected him to dominate and gloat over his victory. This thought humiliated me, and I felt as if a plug had been pulled and all my masculine pride flowed down the drain. Then I had the thought that perhaps my father would not lord it over me this time. This possibility gave me an odd feeling that losing was all right, perhaps even satisfying. Both of our penises were red. My father wore a shirt that was similar to one that you [the therapist] at times wear.

My patient associated the red color of his and his father's penises to that of chimpanzees. Thus an evolutionary perspective was given to the competition for dominance between the patient and his father, and between the patient and myself. Rather than the Oedipal conflict being the cause of the therapeutic competition, the indication was that an archetypal male-male competition for dominance underlay both situations. My patient had lost the fight in the dream, and his feeling of inadequacy was a natural reaction that accompanied the loss, as was the shrinking of his penis; but it was the expectation of domination and gloating by his father that created the fear of extreme humiliation.

Such inner experiences are not ones that a man can be talked out of through reason. Telling a man there is no inherent reason to feel humiliated after he has been bullied negates the validity of an archetypal experience: feeling humiliated and psychologically castrated after domination by another man is an inherent part of a pattern. Similarly, to tell a man it is hubris to feel puffed up after a victory is useless since the increase in testosterone that accompanies the triumph fills the victor with pride and potency. At best, such a victor can be made aware of the requirements of good sportsmanship, which provide the winner of a competition with rules on how to behave in an appropriate manner, for instance, by not gloating and by congratulating the loser on a good effort.

The archetypal dynamic of male-male competition for dominance is a common mythological motif, and mythology also indicates the best way for males to deal with victory and defeat in competitive situations with other males.

In *The Blood-Brother's Saga*, a medieval Icelandic tale, the following destructive interaction takes place:

> Both Thorgeir and Thormod remained that summer at the Strands. All men feared them and the strife they sowed around them like noxious weeds in a field. It is said that once at the height of their pride and insolence, Thorgeir said to Thormod: "Do you know of any other man equal to us in keenness and manhood, and equally tested in deeds of valor?" Thormod replied: "Men could surely be found who are no less brave than we." Then Thorgeir said: "And which of us would overcome the other if we two fought together?" Thormod answered: "That I know not; but I know that this question of yours will put an end to our comradeship and fellowship and that we can no longer go along together." Thorgeir said: "I had not thought at all of trying to see who was the better man of us two." Thormod replied, "You were surely thinking of it while you

spoke, and this will part our fellowship." And this, indeed, was the outcome.[8]

The competitive feelings voiced by Thorgeir are understood by Thormod not just as ones that will indicate who is more capable, but as a competition for dominance. The comparison is made at the "height of their pride and insolence" and after they have equated victory with "keenness and manhood." The loser would be humiliated. That is why Thormod has to end the comradeship.

Another competition for dominance takes place in *The Epic of Gilgamesh*:

> Gilgamesh got up and came to the house. Then Enkidu stepped out, he stood in the street and blocked the way. Mighty Gilgamesh came on and Enkidu met him at the gate. He put out his foot and prevented Gilgamesh from entering the house, so they grappled, holding each other like bulls. They broke the doorposts and the walls shook, they snorted like bulls locked together. They shattered the doorposts and the walls shook. Gilgamesh bent his knee with his foot planted on the ground and with a turn Enkidu was thrown. Then immediately his fury died. When Enkidu was thrown he said to Gilgamesh, "There is not another like you in the world. . . ." So Enkidu and Gilgamesh embraced and their friendship was sealed.[9]

As far as the masculine relationship is concerned, the difference in outcome between the two mythological competitions for dominance is dramatic: one ends in the breaking of a comradeship, the other in friendship. The reason for the difference is critical. Thormod knew that Thorgeir's discussion of competition implied domination and humiliation of the victor by the loser. In the contest between Gilgamesh and Enkidu there is no overt show of domination by the victor or humiliation of the loser. As soon as Gilgamesh wins, his aggression abates and he does not gloat. In turn, Enkidu immediately recognizes Gilgamesh's superiority and praises him. A friendship is sealed.

If male friends are not aware of the proper way to handle this dynamic, competitive situations that naturally arise may cause them to unconsciously act out the need to dominate and ruin the friendship. Awareness, on the other hand, can lead to a conscious acceptance of a fair competition that does not result in gloating by the victor or excess shame by the loser.

A man has to walk a fine line in order to balance the opposition between the desire to dominate his fellow males in competitive situations and his awareness of the sensitivity of the loser's injured masculine pride. Only a man who understands the archetypal energy in male-male competition for dominance and who can give playful and creative vent to his competitive relationship with other men can walk that line in his relationships.

It is especially important for fathers to be conscious of the dynamic of male-male competition for dominance in relationship to their sons. It is easy for fathers to consciously or unconsciously dominate and humiliate their sons. The son needs to feel the urge to compete with the father—competition is an attribute of the traditional masculine gender role—but he must not be humiliated by the father's superior power. Domination and humiliation by fathers are major reasons that sons feel inadequate in their masculinity and develop, as a defense, the exaggerated masculinity of machismo.

The father needs to be conscious not only of the dynamic of male-male competition for dominance but also of the son's need to submit to the father as mentor and guide. In the previous dream, the competitive loss to his father caused a feeling of inadequacy in the son and a shrinking of his penis, but there was also a satisfaction that came from being with a dominant male, so long as the victor did not lord it over him. A father needs to be aware of his own urge to submit and its relationship to transformation in order to be sensitive to a son's ambivalent relationship to the opposition of dominance and submission: the son wants to be able to submit to a dominant male as mentor and, at the same time, be a dominant male in competitive situations with other males. It is by embodying the powerful mentor role for his son, as well as, ironically, exploring the expressive/passive dimension in himself, that a father can help his son grow into the masculine gender role.

3 | The Man and the Mask
The Development of the Masculine Persona

As we have seen, the tendency to develop roles is archetypal. The particular archetype that mediates the relationship between a man and his society Jung called the *persona*. Like all archetypes, the persona represents a tendency to form an image under certain circumstances. Also like all archetypes, the particular image that is formed is culturally determined.

The persona is a social construct. It deals with a man or woman in relationship to others, either in reality or in fantasy. The persona has to do with a man's experience of himself in the eyes of another. On the basis of the social norms that have been integrated, a man imagines what the situation requires of him, what the social rules and demands are, and then decides whether or not to present himself according to those requirements. The persona is a series of adaptations—the way in which the ego adapts and presents itself to the environment.

While the development of a persona is an archetypal "necessity" in which a man can be more or less successful, identifying with the persona can be a roadblock on the path to psychological balance. A person may believe that he actually *is* as he presents himself, and as others see him.

The persona represents a limited way of being human. Even if we were to take all the various personae a man develops—professional, husband, parent, and so on—much of what he potentially could be is not included. In this sense, while the

persona is real, it is also a "false self" in that it is not a complete reflection of a man's individuality. The persona's falseness
is problematic, however, only insofar as the man's ego identifies
with it. The more rigid the persona and the identification, the
more that which is spontaneously true about the man is suppressed.

When I was young I drove a man's car cross-country and
delivered it to his house in New Jersey. I had never met the
man before and, since he was not home when I delivered the
car, his wife invited me to await her husband's return and share
dinner with their family. The man turned out to be a wealthy
and successful doctor and teacher at a medical school. I was
struck to hear everybody at the dinner table, not just the servants, but even his wife and children, address him as "Doctor"!
He, and all around him, had identified the man with his persona. I was able to see no hint of this man's individuality outside of his formal persona of "Doctor."

In summing up the persona, Jung said:

> When we analyse the persona we strip off the mask, and
> discover that what seemed to be individual is at bottom
> collective; in other words, that the persona was only a
> mask of the collective psyche. Fundamentally the persona is
> nothing real: it is a compromise between individual and so-
> ciety as to what a man should appear to be. He takes a
> name, earns a title, exercises a function, he is this or that.
> In a certain sense all this is real, yet in relation to the es-
> sential individuality of the person concerned it is only a
> secondary reality, a compromise formation, in making
> which others often have a greater share than he. The per-
> sona is a semblance, a two-dimensional reality, to give it a
> nickname.[1]

THE AMERICAN MASCULINE PERSONA

The qualities considered masculine and feminine differ in Western society in many ways from those in other societies and, on a superficial level, even fluctuate within society. Women, for example, generally have longer hair than men and wear skirts and dresses. In American society, however, young men effected a style of long hair during the 1960s, and it is currently common for women to wear pants. Similarly, masculine and feminine roles vary within American society across individual, economic, cultural, and ethnic lines. The masculine and feminine gender roles in a well-educated upper-middle-class household differ from those of a working-class environment. In addition, there are many gender subroles: the masculine gender role, for instance, has subroles related to work, family, sexuality, intimacy, affective communication, and the status of the individual. Despite such variability, however, gender roles are relatively rigid. Norms exist, and although minor deviations from the norm are allowed, major changes from the norm cannot occur without consequences.

Various researchers have explored the American masculine gender role in detail.[2] Their approach has typically been to survey men from different occupations and phases of life and ask them to explain what characteristics they associated with males and females. The writers found that almost all of the men in their samples experienced a sharp polarity between masculinity and femininity. The characteristics the men considered masculine paralleled those of the instrumental/active dimension, and the qualities associated to the feminine coincided with the expressive/passive dimension.

As clear as men are about what qualities characterize their

masculinity, they are equally clear about what the opposite polarity, femininity, is like. Since men define themselves by what they are not (they are nothing like women) as much as by what they are, it is often easier to understand what American men consider masculine by first describing the characteristics men attribute to women. Femininity—that is, nonmasculinity—is associated with expressiveness and passivity: Women are ruled by emotions and feelings; they are likely to make decisions on the basis of feelings and intuition rather than careful analysis. Women are weak, frail, submissive, and lack assertion; they prefer to take a passive position toward those who have more power and do not like to act aggressively. Women are nurturant; they want a home, to build a nest, and to take care of the needs of their husbands and children.

By contrast, according to the men, being masculine means being instrumental and active: a leader, confident and self-reliant, nonexpressive of feelings, logical and rational, competitive, ambitious, and successful in one's work.

High achievement and ambition to be successful in one's work are hallmarks of the masculine gender role. Men are expected to be successful, seek higher status, and be looked up to. American men must achieve wealth, fame, or recognition. The acquisition of material goods is one of the external manifestations of success, and by its emphasis men can be sure that others are aware of their success. The striving for success and status underscores the importance of competition in men's lives.

It is often easier to grasp a norm when it is presented in an extreme form. Since the instrumental/active norms characteristic of the masculine gender role often appear in an exaggerated manner in males who have psychological conflicts about masculinity, I will use clinical vignettes to illustrate my description of the gender role common to American males.

AN EXAMPLE: JIM

Jim, a man in his forties, started therapy after his wife asked him for a divorce. She claimed that Jim drank too much, verbally abused her and the children, would not communicate, and refused to get treatment for his depression. After his wife threatened to leave him, Jim's lifelong depression deepened and he developed suicidal thoughts.

Jim spent the first few months of therapy talking about his father and the damage he felt his father had done to Jim's feelings about himself as a man. His father was an alcoholic who, especially when drunk, would mock Jim's masculinity. He would try to provoke his young son to fight and then laugh at the tears with which Jim responded. The father would torment Jim further with disparaging remarks such as "fairy" and "queer." Growing up under such painful conditions, Jim compensated for his wounded masculine self-image by developing a masculine persona wedded to the values of success, wealth, and status.

Jim experienced the relationship between achievement, wealth, and masculinity most strongly in his career. He had become a very successful financial investor. Not only did his career earn him a great deal of money, but his specialty of "shorting" the stock market—essentially a form of high-risk gambling that the stock market would decline—he considered further indication of masculine daring. While his career as an investor and money manager did not give Jim intrinsic pleasure, his concerns about masculine adequacy were mitigated by his taking risks, making a lot of money, and being in a position of power over the nearly fifty people he supervised. Jim spent the money he earned, not on things he really needed or enjoyed, but on objects that had prestige and that indicated that he was a successful person, worthy of masculine respect: fancy clothes, expensive restaurants, and powerful automobiles.

Jim had a "Hemingway" type of masculine persona. He had read Hemingway as an adolescent and considered his exploits, especially as a fisherman, indicative of a "true" masculinity. In an attempt to emulate his masculine ideal, Jim now owned a large and expensive fishing boat replete with the most expensive deep-sea fishing gear. Owning the boat reinforced his exaggerated masculine persona, even though Jim became violently seasick the moment he was out of sight of land. Consequently, Jim would spend weekends on the boat, showing it off to friends and colleagues, but he and the boat never left the marina.

Having power, exercising control over others, and being recognized as a leader are related to achievement. Power is a masculine prerogative in our society. It is a direct result of success—the more success, the more power. The masculine drive toward achievement is characterized by an active striving for power rather than a general thrust to achieve for personal satisfaction, even if the achievement does not bring power.

Jim generalized the relationship between masculinity, achievement, and power not only to his career but to almost every area of his life, especially to women and sexuality. During his marriage Jim had many affairs. He equated sex with conquest, and the more women he had sex with, the more powerful he considered himself; he was powerful not only over the women he conquered but also over the men he had beat out in order to get the women. In Jim's mind he was always competing with other men over who could perform better and give the women greater sexual satisfaction. He considered the need for bodily pleasures feminine and was concerned that giving in to such a need would indicate to the other person that they could affect him and control him. Consequently, Jim was almost never interested in his own sexual pleasure as he concentrated almost exclusively on how long he could maintain an erection and whether he could "give" the woman an orgasm, two aspects of intercourse that Jim considered indicative of masculine power. His insecurity about his masculinity would surface, invariably, after intercourse, when he would compulsively question his partner about her past lovers and how well his performance compared.

Strength, toughness, stamina, and the ability to endure bodily stress are other important criteria of the masculine gender role in American society. Men carry themselves with an air of confidence and self-reliance at all times. No matter what the stress, the man is expected to stand up to it and survive, or go down fighting. Part of the image is inexpressiveness, a refusal to show evidence of fear or vulnerability. Daring, violence, aggression, and risk taking are aspects of this role.

Jim's identification with this tough aspect of the masculine persona was brought home to him by an incident that occurred about one year after he started therapy. Jim was a large, athletic man who liked to imagine himself as a tough street fighter, but in fact, he had never been in a fight in his life. One day he and his wife were walking down a busy avenue in New York City. On the avenue they encountered a group of boisterous teenagers who were making nasty remarks to the passersby. As Jim and his wife walked by, the teenagers made comments not only disparaging to him but sexually suggestive to his wife. Rather than just going on his way, Jim felt a "masculine embarrassment" and began to yell at the teenagers, who in turn became physically menacing. Only the common sense of his wife, who dragged him away, saved Jim from bodily harm.

When Jim told me of the incident at our next session, I asked him why he had not just kept on walking by the teenagers. He responded that he had felt ashamed to not behave in a "tough and fearless" manner in front of his wife. Anything other than a show of bravado would have been "passive and womanly," and he imagined that his wife would have lost respect for him.

Being logical, analytical, and intellectually competent are other significant characteristics of the male gender role. Men use logic as opposed to emotion. They adopt an affectively neutral, achievement-oriented, and rational attitude toward external situations; they inhibit their emotions toward others. The man is expected to solve all problems rationally. Even if he has actually responded emotionally, he will often deny emotion as the basis of his decision and make up a rationalization that appears to be logical.

The inhibition of emotion and the need to appear logical helped explain why Jim had been so reluctant to seek psychological treatment from his chronic, debilitating depression. For years Jim's wife had implored him to get help, not only for his own sake, but also for the benefit of their marriage and children. Jim would not hear of it; he considered it "unmanly" to admit to suffering from emotional problems. Jim considered getting help from others a "female thing." It would have been all right with him for his wife to seek professional help to aid their marital problems, but Jim adamantly refused to get any treatment for himself. He could handle his emotions by himself, he would angrily declare.

Jim would make up rational reasons to "explain" his irrational symptoms. For instance, when he cried uncontrollably over the loss of a hankie, he rationalized that the hankie was an old favorite and thus justified his irrational emotional response. Rather than admit that he had a psychological problem, Jim handled his conflict in the way men traditionally handle their feelings—by drinking too much alcohol, and being cranky and irritable with his wife and verbally abusive toward his children. Jim finally admitted to his emotional problems and sought treatment only after his wife asked for a divorce and he became frightened by suicidal urges.

THE DEVELOPMENT OF THE MASCULINE PERSONA

As we discussed in the first chapter, the archetypal event fundamental to the development of consciousness is the differentiation of psychic reality into oppositional categories, the most significant of which, for gender development, are the categories masculine–feminine and the dimensions instrumental/active–expressive/passive.

At around three to five years of age, the young boy realizes that he belongs to the masculine category and seeks to acquire the attributes that will cause him to feel like a competent male, adequate and esteemed in the eyes of his family and society. At the same time, he tries to avoid becoming what he knows he is not—a female. To this end, the young boy seeks out and tries to integrate into his persona the characteristics that his society and culture indicate are appropriate to his gender. In American society, the characteristics of the masculine gender role are coincidental with the instrumental/active dimension.

For the young boy, the major psychological process involved in the development of his gender role is identification with males whom the boy considers models of masculinity. The social processes involved are direct tutelage by significant others on how to be masculine and feedback in the form of praise and criticism.

SOCIAL LEARNING

According to social-learning theorists, the major mechanisms in the acquisition of distinctive gender features are a combination of observational learning and direct tutelage.[3]

Children observe, watch, listen, and learn. They watch parents and significant others, such as mass media personalities and public figures, and choose models to imitate. A number of factors appear to determine the likelihood that a child will choose a specific person as a role model. First, the more available the adult, the more apt that person is to be chosen as a role model; mothers are usually more available than fathers. The more powerful the adult, the more apt a child is to model its behavior on this person; fathers are usually experienced as more powerful in the family than mothers. Children are likely to model themselves after adults whom they see as having qualities similar to themselves. Finally, children tend to choose nurturant adults as models.

In addition, parents have somewhat different expectations about appropriate behaviors for boys and girls and directly and indirectly teach their male and female children to behave differently. Even before birth the gender role is molded by the parent's fantasies, with their expectations and behavioral proscriptions. After birth these fantasies intensify with the color of nursery clothes and the kinds of toys purchased. Biological and temperamental traits that fit the traditional roles are praised; those that do not are discouraged.

Language plays an important part in learning gender roles. Words provide distinctive features for gender roles, and parents use verbal cues to shape the child's behavior toward the role expected of them. By using language to label behaviors and feelings as masculine or feminine, the child's knowledge of gender roles is increased. Statements and commands to the child about what he or she should or should not do encourage and discourage different behaviors and feelings in males and females.

Emotion also plays a part. Praise and criticism not only provide information about what is appropriate and inappropriate but also endow behavior related to gender roles with positive and negative affect. Pride induced for appropriate gender role behavior or shame aroused for wrong behavior results in anxiety over deviation from conventional norms.

I will use the image of the inexpressive male as an example of how social-learning processes influence the development of the masculine persona.

Male inexpressiveness is based on a lifelong socialization process that begins in infancy, when girls are taught to act feminine and to desire feminine objects and boys are taught how to be masculine. Boys quickly learn that masculinity is expressed largely through physical courage, toughness, competitiveness, and aggressiveness, whereas the expression of feelings and emotions is feminine. If the boy is too gentle, expressive, or responsive he runs the distinct danger of being ridiculed, ostracized, or physically punished.

One study demonstated nearly twenty years ago that if families press these demands early in childhood and frequently enforce them harshly, by the time male children reach kindergarten, many feel virtual panic at being caught doing anything traditionally defined as feminine.[4]

We are all familiar with experiences, either our own or observed, of grown-ups admonishing a young boy who has been hurt and is crying that boys are not supposed to express such emotions. Sometimes there is even the more shaming pejorative "sissy" thrown at the boy, or he is told that only girls cry and he should be a man. By attaching shame and humiliation to the expression of emotions, parents solidify the idea in their son that a real man does not show his emotions and that outward expressions of emotions are feminine and undesirable in a man.

Pressure to conform does not have to come primarily from the immediate family to have its effect; the social environment can be a harsh teacher and enforcer of gender norms. As the male child moves out of the family container into male peer groups, the taboo against expressing feelings characteristic of females can be intense. According to studies of male subcultures in schools, street corner male groups, and delinquent gangs, to be affectionate, gentle, and compassionate toward others is not to be one of the boys. It is to be a sissy, to misplay the male role.[5]

The mass media convey a similar message. The image of the male role does not usually include affecionate, gentle, tender or soft-hearted behavior. Such feelings are certainly not expressed. Two basic types of inexpressive male common in the media are the cowboy and the playboy.[6] An example of the cowboy is the strong, silent John Wayne type of hero. While he likes females and has feelings toward them, he does not express his feelings. The James Bond playboy type is similar to the cowboy in his detachment and inexpressiveness. He differs in that he is nonfeeling toward women and treats them more as objects to be used. Of course, neither cowboy nor playboy expresses feelings toward men, except the emotion considered most masculine— anger. Tenderness and affection toward other men would bring up the danger of appearing nonmasculine or, even worse, homosexual.

Confronted by models in the family, peer groups, and mass media that instruct the suppression of feelings and praise and criticism to ensure conformity to the norm, the young male quickly and firmly learns that the expression of feelings and emotions is not compatible with the masculine role. Being nonexpressive, on the other hand, is considered a positive sign of masculinity. The exceptions to this rule are anger, resentment, and violence, whose expression is sanctioned as part of the masculine role.

I might add that the inexpressive masculine persona is so ingrained that it is not even thought about. It is a role that has been so thoroughly learned that it is taken for granted by the individual and the culture. Being inexpressive is not even considered a role, it is an assumed reality—men really are this way, it is the nature of masculinity.

Practically speaking, such a socialization process renders many men unable to recognize and express basic feelings and emotional needs. Inner conflict and interpersonal misunderstanding and frustration often result. For instance, the expression of an emotional need for love and affection is opposed to the male gender role of self-sufficiency and independence. As a consequence, many men consider such emotional needs to be a sign of weakness and do not develop a conscious relationship to them; either they do not recognize their needs or they are too humiliated to state them and ask for their satisfaction. To save themselves the embarrassment of indicating that they have emotional needs, men often expect the women in their lives to read their minds and satisfy their needs without their having to express themselves. Men may get confused and upset if the woman does not accommodate, because they understand this to mean that the woman is not fulfilling her gender role of relatedness. Their confusion often leads to hurt and anger, which they also cannot admit, because doing so would necessitate recognizing that they have been hurt, something real men do not do.

IDENTIFICATION

To identify with someone means to make yourself similar to the other person. The person who identifies begins to think, feel, and act as he imagines the other person would. In addition to identifying with others, people also identify with parts of their own personality, mistaking the part for the whole. For instance, a man may identify himself with his masculine persona and become unaware that he is larger and more inclusive than that structure. Since one of the primary people that a boy identifies with is his father, we can use the concept of identification to explore the issue of the father's significance for the development of the son's masculine persona.

Jung differentiated imitation from identification. He said that imitation was a process of conscious copying, whereas identification was an unconscious imitation.[7] In the course of development people meet obstacles that they cannot easily master, and identification can provide a useful way to deal with the situation as another person would. But identification can also hinder development if the person relies on its use even when a more individual adaptation to a situation is possible. A person then arrives at a solution or attitude only because it was the way another person would, rather than coming to his own conclusions. In addition, since identification is an unconscious process, the person does not know that his attitude has come from another. The result is a loss of separateness and an alienation from one's individuality. When a son identifies with his father, for instance, the son adopts the father's way of behaving, and the son becomes the same as the father and not a separate individual.

Jung considered identification to be a generally regressive phenomenon—that is, rather than adapting to a new situation in a unique way, the person goes back to an earlier form of adaptation modeled on a parent. In terms of gender development, the son might come up against some problem in adaptation and wonder how a man is supposed to deal with it. Rather than trying to develop an attitude that would enable him to master the situation as an individual, the son might unconsciously regress to an earlier state of identification with his father and solve the situation as his father would. For example, a boy might have a disagreement with another boy and wonder how to resolve the conflict in accordance with his masculine role. If the boy regresses to an identification with a father who was pugnacious, the boy might deal with the current conflict by becoming overly aggressive and trying to dominate the other boy. In such an instance, the son does not develop competence in his own masculine gender role; instead, he disguises himself in his father's gender role. The unconscious motive for the son's identification, according to Jung, would be some inability or unwillingness to face up to and adapt to a current problem as an individual.

Whereas Jung considered identification to be an attempt to unconsciously solve the problem of an external adaptation, Freud considered identification to be a defense mechanism—a way of holding in check an internal conflict that might cause anxiety. If a boy fears his angry father, for instance, the boy can control his anxiety by identifying with the father and imagining himself to be similar to the frightening father.

Since classical psychoanalysis, as developed originally by Freud, has been extremely influential in affecting the way we think about the development of the masculine gender role, I will elaborate on it in some detail.

In developing his theory about how men become masculine and women feminine, Freud stressed underlying bisexuality, the role of the anatomy, the resolution of the Oedipus complex, and the mechanism of identification.

In Freud's nineteenth-century Vienna, the generally prevalent view was that boys were innately more aggressive and self-sufficient and girls more affectionate and compliant. In opposition to that view, Freud took the position of biological and psychological bisexuality. The observed differences, he contended, were not innate but due to the effects of social customs; for instance, men appeared more aggressive than women because social customs inhibited women's aggression and forced them into passive situations.

According to Freud, at around two to three years of age children enter the Oedipal phase of development and the paths between boys and girls diverge. He contended that the discovery that boys have a penis and girls do not has far-reaching consequences for subsequent psychological development, especially for gender distinctions. The discovery of the anatomical distinction largely accounts for how boys and girls develop out of their childhood bisexual disposition into adult males and females.

Freud's theory of the Oedipal phase of development centers around desirous feelings for the parent of the opposite sex and aggressive, competitive feelings toward the parent of the same sex. For example, the boy associates the pleasurable genital sensations he feels with a desire for an exclusive relationship with mother. Along with the yearnings for mother go wishes for the annihilation of any rivals, generally the father and any siblings. But these murderous wishes arouse conflicts in the child that center around a fear of retaliation, specifically a fantasy of castration. In addition to such fears of paternal retaliation, the thought of eliminating the father raises in the son feelings of guilt, dependency, and insecurity at the prospect of losing the father's support and care. Most often the conflict between the wishful impulse and the fears associated with acting on it is resolved. The boy's fear is repressed—forced into the unconscious—and the hostile impulses are replaced by a desire to be like the father. The identification with his father marks the beginning of the boy's active acquisition of masculinity; he begins to want to learn how to become a man.

The situation is actually more complicated than this schematic presentation indicates, owing to the boy's inherent bisexuality. The Oedipus complex has a double orientation, active and passive, the relative strength of whose components affect subsequent gender identifications. If a strong feminine component is present, for instance, its strength is increased by the threat to the boy's masculinity, and he may then fall into an identification with his mother.

The boy's identification with his father's masculine role is also dependent on his relationship to the father. If the natural fear and aggression inherent in the Oedipal situation is complicated by an actual dominating, competitive father-son relationship, the boy may withdraw into a defiant attitude that rejects the father's masculinity, or, on the contrary, into a brittle identification with the aggressor.

Although Freud recognized early identifications based on love, he saw the main motive for identification in fears of loss and retaliation. Both male and female infants fear loss of love of the mother, the primary supplier of their needs and the first person with whom they identify. During the Oedipal stage the process changes for boys, and their identifications become primarily motivated by their fear of the father.

A number of problems bedevil classical psychoanalytic identification theory as an explanation for the development of the masculine persona.

For Freud, the difference between the gender development of males and females was a consequence of the anatomical distinction between their genitals. The boy realizes that he has a penis and females do not. He imagines that females once had a penis and lost it in some manner, an eventuality that could befall him at the hands of his father. The threat of castration causes the boy to give up his wish for the mother and identify with his father and develop his masculine role.

Available research, however, suggests that young children do not differentiate males from females on the basis of external genitalia. As a matter of fact, one study found that 88 percent of three-year-olds, 69 percent of four-year-olds, 49 percent of five-year-olds, and 30 percent of six-year-olds could not distinguish between male and female external genitalia.[8] Yet by the time children are four to six years old, they already have developed gender stereotypes: fathers are perceived as more powerful, punitive, aggressive, and instrumentally competent, whereas mothers are perceived as more nurturant.[9] That children are still confused about genital differences at an age when they clearly stereotype gender roles in terms of size, strength, aggression, and power strongly suggests that genital concepts do not form the direct basis for these other connotations of gender differences.

The significance of the defense mechanism of identification with the aggressor has been overemphasized as a process involved in the development of gender roles. While the defense mechanism may play a significant part in the neurotic development of masculinity, classical psychoanalytic theory neglects the more common and significant identifications based on love and imitation.[10]

Freud's theory assumes the primacy of masculinity. Both the boy and girl begin their sexual life with a masculine erogenous zone—the penis: an actual penis for the boy and a penis equivalent (clitoris) for the girl. Freud said: "We are now obliged to recognize that the little girl is a little man."[11] Part of the girl's task in her passage from masculine to feminine, according to Freud, is to hand over the sensitivity from her clitoris to her vagina.

We now have plenty of evidence to contradict Freud's assumption of the primacy of the male anatomy, however.[12] The developing fetus will take on a female form, despite the original chromosomal sexual assignment, unless there is a well-timed intrusion of the male hormone. It appears that, rather than the female anatomy being that of a defective male, the anatomy of the male, in contrast to biblical cosmogony, is a modification built on the basic feminine form.

Even after we discount his misplaced emphasis on the male anatomy in the development of gender roles, Freud's assertion of an underlying bisexuality nevertheless holds up well, as does his recognition that most of the observed psychological differences between males and females are not biologically innate but determined by psychosocial development.

Conclusions

When a boy, at approximately three to five years of age, comes to discriminate the category male from the category female, this splitting of psychic reality into opposites, an archetypal event in itself, stimulates the persona archetype. The boy then seeks information in order to fill out the gender aspect of the persona. Because his father and mother stand as representatives of the two categories, the son will realize that he and his father share the category of "maleness," and that the category of "femaleness" is one to which the boy cannot belong. Observation and direct tutelage by agents of society will aid the boy as he goes about learning how to be a male—that is, the masculine gender role. Praise and other reinforcements let the boy know that his need to feel competent as a male is succeeding, and his self-esteem will increase. Identifying with the father and other male models will also foster the development of his masculine persona, as will avoiding being like the mother and other female models.

Sociocultral, familial, and individual factors largely determine the unique way in which each male develops a persona and whether or not he fixates at some point in the process. A family climate of warmth, expressiveness, security, integration of conflict, and high social participation, for instance, facilitates masculine gender role development. An admired, loving father leads to a desire for the boy to identify and aids the boy in becoming a man; a home life that values the mother and traditional feminine values aids the subsequent healing of the masculine-feminine split. Such a climate allows for the exploration and integration of the new and the problematic. A disturbed family environment, characterized by coldness, hostility, anxiety, and conflict, on the other hand, leads to defensivenss, fixations, disturbed images of masculinity, and pathological developmental trends.

The persona that develops can be either secure or brittle for many reasons. The culture may hold up a model of masculinity that is commensurate with the individual male's psychological or physical nature. A tall, muscular, athletic male will feel adequate if he identifies with the image of masculinity largely propagated in American culture. A man who is constitutionally nonaggressive, on the other hand, may experience inadequacy as a consequence of not conforming to societal standards. The absence of appropriate male models, domination by the father or the mother, and belittlement can undermine a male's sense of masculine adequacy. To overcome feelings of inadequacy, the persona often develops as a defensive overcompensation of the traditional masculine role, so that masculine characteristics and values appear in an exaggerated form. Other times, major components of the masculine role remain undeveloped, and the male continues to suffer feelings of masculine inadequacy.

The development of an adequate masculine persona—the characteristics of the instrumental/active dimension—is critical for the male. Competence in that dimension is the route to collective acceptance, value, and feelings of adequacy. Identification with the persona is also a danger, however; it results in a loss of individuality. Rather than developing into his own person, the boy becomes a replica of his masculine role model (typically his father) and the collective that his role model represents.

Jung and Freud both used the concept of identification to explain the boy's internalizing his father's masculinity in the development of his own masculine gender role. Both of their viewpoints can be criticized for their failure to appreciate the teleological significance of the identification with the father for the gender role development of the son. Jung saw identification with the father as a regressive step, Freud as a defensive process that controls fear of the father's aggression. In both instances, the son's individuality is compromised.

Neither Jung nor Freud recognized the progressive aspect of identification with the father. It is an example of the son's active attempt to seek his masculine gender role through identification with appropriate models. The process has a conscious purpose: the son knowingly strives to imitate the characteristics of his father in order to develop his masculine persona. It has an unconscious purpose as well: the incorporation of the father as a guiding male image is an initial but essential step in a teleological process whose goal is wholeness. Identification with a father, or an appropriate surrogate, who has an adequate masculine gender role must be successfully accomplished before the boy can fulfill the fundamental and necessary prerequisite for development toward becoming a male human being. The boy needs first to satisfy the requirement of being an adequate male in the eyes of his sociocultural milieu. To that end, the boy must acquire and integrate the characteristics of the instrumental/active dimension, the hallmark of traditional masculinity.

A similar criticism applies to the social-learning view of the development of gender roles. Social-learning theory conceives of the boy as acted on and shaped by the environment. The boy observes his milieu and imitates the mother or the father depending on such variables as power, availability, and nurturance. The child refines his image of masculinity and receives information from his parents, through reward and punishment, about whether his attempts to differentiate the masculine and feminine roles is correct.

Left out of the social-learning picture is the purposefulness of the process. The boy actively seeks to learn his gender role so that he can become the man he knows he is meant to be. The boy imitates the father, not because he is rewarded for the learning, but because he realizes that he and his father belong to the same category. When the son receives praise for being like his father, the son feels proud that his competence as a male has been recognized and confirmed. Reward and punish-

ment serve merely as feedback; praise lets the boy know that
he is gaining competence in his desired direction, criticism in-
forms him that he has taken a wrong turn. Praise and criticism
are merely signposts that demarcate the forks in the road of
the journey the boy has begun. Of primary importance is the
boy's search for a goal—a sense of what it means to be a man,
a step on the journey to the as yet unconscious question of
what it means to be a male human being.

4 | My Father, My Self
Identification and Conflict

Early psychoanalytic writers were primarily interested in exploring the father's effect on his children during the Oedipal phase of development. They concluded that the child experienced the father as an intrusion into an exclusive mother-child relationship, a figure who required the child to renounce the mother as love object and acknowledge paternal authority. Even when subsequent writers turned their attention to the years prior to the Oedipal phase, they continued to emphasize the father's negative aspects. The child was still thought to experience the father as an intruder into its state of oral bliss and intimacy with the mother. As a consequence of such early experiences, these writers concluded that the child experienced the father as fundamentally a hostile figure who was to be fought or submitted to, a figure who was irrevocably tinged with fear and aggression.

Subsequent research has indicated that a more positive role exists for the father. The father's role in helping the child separate from its early relationship to the mother is vital, but the role is not, as originally thought, that of a threatening figure who forces the child out of the relationship with the mother. Rather, the father's importance lies in his ability to offer himself as a loving alternative who draws the child into the external reality the child is meant to enter.

An implicit opposition lies between the child's need to develop and move into the reality of the world outside mother and the child's need for comfort. An urge to develop coexists with the pain of separation. While the mother represents a "home base" to return to for comfort and security, she also can represent eternal dependency, the pull toward infantilism, and loss of individuality.

Against the threatening possibility of comfortable dependency stands the powerful paternal force. An early identification with that force, which precedes the frustration and hostility of the Oedipal phase, leads into the real world of things and people. The positive father represents not a threatening or frustrating presence but a guide into a reality that can be related to with playful and adaptive mastery.

The father, as the natural "other," belongs to the new and exciting nonmother world. He helps the child to differentiate from the mother by representing the world that the child is entering when the child, as part of a normal developmental sequence, separates from the merged relationship with the mother. If the father is receptive and supportive as the child moves away from the mother, the world will seem like a safer place. The father offers the child a stable place in which to practice independence and separateness. The very concept of reality is represented by the father, that is, reality experienced as an external force.

The father's importance as a positive, nonthreatening figure who attracts the child into external reality is indicated by research on attachment behavior. During the first year of life, children show stronger attachment behaviors toward the mother but have a more affiliative relationship with the father.[1] Attachment behaviors, such as crying and asking to be held, are more directly useful in promoting proximity and contact. Affiliative behaviors, such as smiling and vocalizing, on the other hand, are employed in friendly interactions with people regardless of whether they are attached. In addition, twelve- to twenty-one-month-old children protest when left alone and explore little during parental absence, yet few protest separation from either parent when the other parent remains with them.[2]

This research indicates that a positive relationship with the father can provide the security the child needs in order to separate from the mother and explore the environment. As a matter of fact, it is the affiliative behavior characteristic of the interaction with the father that most encourages the development of the child's ability to engage the external world in new relationships.

For the development of gender roles, the father is especially important in attracting the child into a positive relationship to the reality that exists outside mother. Like females, the boy's initial identifications are with the mother. The father enters the picture as the primary representative of the outer world, who defines what is an acceptable gender role. He emphasizes by his very presence that there is a way to be—masculine—that differs from the initial identification with the mother's way of being—feminine. Except in cases of an absent father, the mother has far less effect than the father on the development of the boy's gender role.[3]

The father does not intrude into the mother-son situation, as was initially thought by the psychoanalysts, nor is implicit threat necessary to cause the boy to separate from his initial identification with his mother; the boy's movement from mother to father is not a defense based on fear of the father. Rather, as part of a normal process of development the boy recognizes that he is a male and looks to the environment for a model with which to identify so that he can find a way to become the male being he already knows he is. The boy becomes aware of the father as a male like himself and includes the father in a "we-males" category. The boy recognizes the father as the more competent member of the category, and he gives the father the implicit authority to define the masculine gender role. While male siblings, peers, and other adults also become part of the "we-males" category and can be quite influential in the development of a boy's gender role, the most significant identification figure in the development of the masculine gender role is the father. The significance of the father is not as a cause of masculine development but as a facilitator and, perhaps even more important, as the person who determines the quality of the son's relationship to his masculinity. Whether the son is secure or defensive in his gender role will be mostly determined by who his father is and the quality of their relationship.

The son's identification with his father's masculinity can be either developmental or defensive. Developmental identification is the normal process by which the son looks to the father for the provision of a model on which to pattern himself. The basis for developmental identification is a nurturing parent-child relationship that motivates the child to consciously emulate and unconsciously incorporate—that is, develop an internal image of—the beloved parent. The son wants to be a man, and he wants to be a man just like his father. Defensive identification, on the other hand, is not based on love and affection, but is synonymous with identification with the aggressor. It is a way of reducing anxiety by becoming like the person one is afraid of.

Research indicates that whether a male's masculinity is based on defensive or developmental identifications is related to paternal nurturance and paternal participation in limit setting and decision making. Paternal nurturance refers to the father's affectionate, attentive encouragement of his child. The boy wants to be like the father he loves and who loves and supports him. Similarly, the son's perception of his father's authority through the father's participation in family decisions and the setting of limits leads to a developmental identification with a powerful and valued figure. Taken separately, no one of these factors is sufficient to ensure that a boy will become masculine. All three—a powerful masculine image, family involvement, and basic affection—are necessary.[4]

Men who develop an insecure or defensive masculinity, on the other hand, often grow up in situations with a nonnurturing father who is either passive and ineffectual or dominating. One study found that adolescent boys low in masculine interest often came from homes in which the father played a traditionally feminine role.[5] The fathers of these boys took over activities such as cooking and household chores and generally did not participate in family decision making or limit setting. What seemed to inhibit the boys' masculine development was not their father's participation in traditionally feminine activities per se, but the fathers' general passivity in family interactions and decision making.

AN EXAMPLE: JAKE

Jake was twenty-five years old when he first came to therapy. He had first gone to an older female therapist, but after a few months found that he was unable to be open with her. This inability was not due to anything the therapist did; her age and her silent approach filled Jake with the fear that she was thinking critical thoughts and would at any moment humiliate him.

While Jake's fear of humiliation was general, he was especially sensitive about his masculinity. Jake was a large, athletic, and handsome young man, but from his stooped shoulders to his flaccid handshake he exhibited passivity. He had recently been rejected by his girlfriend for his ambivalence toward the relationship and a general inability to decide what he wanted to do with his life. Jake said that he was anxious about sex and that his girlfriend had accused him of not being able to thrust into her during intercourse. Jake said that he knew he was a male, but did not feel very secure in his masculinity, nor really what he meant when he used the term *masculine*.

In discussing his background, it soon became clear that Jake had grown up in an environment especially pernicious to the development of his masculine gender role. His mother was the most powerful person in the family. But it was not her authority that was the problem, it was her domination of the household in a very punitive way. Jake's mother was severe and nonpermissive in matters of toilet training, politeness, and sex play. For instance, Jake was toilet trained before he was eighteen months old, and any subsequent slip met a humiliating tirade by his mother. He was always required to sit at the table with both hands folded, never to say a word unless he was first spoken to, and not to leave the table until everyone was finished. A failure to say "thank you" or "please" was cause for a severe punishment. Sex was especially controlled by his mother. As a young child, Jake's mother would slap his hand and tell him he was a "dirty pig" whenever he touched his genitals. When he reached adolescence, she ranted about masturbation.

At first Jake turned to his father, a farmer, for protection. The father was a kind man who at first was affectionate with Jake. Jake recalled an early admiration for his father, following him around the farm pretending to do the same chores. The father was physically large, and Jake imagined him to be as strong inside as he was outside. Unfortunately for Jake, however, his father was quite passive and completely unable to deal with his wife's emotional tirades.

Jake's father initially tried to intercede between his wife and Jake, telling her that her abuse and control of her son was wrong. But he could not stand up to her when she turned her attack on him. Finally, he submitted to her demand that she be declared correct in her treatment of Jake. After this defeat, the father stayed out in the fields or the barn more and more and withdrew from any involvement in the house or Jake. Jake was left to the mercy of his mother.

The mother's cruel dominance combined with the father's passivity had many effects on Jake's development, but in terms of his masculine gender role Jake was especially damaged. Jake understood from visiting at his friend's homes and from what he learned in school that the extreme female dominance in his family was deviant. He was ashamed of his father, who provided a weak, unattractive figure with which to identify. Furthermore, the masculine role itself was experienced by Jake as lacking in value. Every time Jake's mother saw him behaving in a way that was typically masculine—for instance, when Jake would try to behave in a forceful or competent manner—she put him down and told Jake he was weak and incompetent like his father and all other men. This abuse not only damaged Jake's feelings about himself and his father, but it also made it difficult for Jake to find alternative male figures to identify with as a substitute for his father.

In therapy, Jake quickly realized that one consequence of his upbringing was that he was ashamed of being a male and had avoided developing in himself the traditional masculine qualities. In addition, if he did not display masculine qualities Jake presented less of a target for ridicule. Thus, rather than assertion, he exhibited passivity; rather than decisiveness, ambivalence. Thrusting sexually would have given his ex-girlfriend the opportunity to laugh at his potency, so Jake would lie limp underneath her. In Jake's mind, if he did not try to be masculine then his mother—and by extension, other females—would not have an opportunity to attack and make fun of his masculine persona.

THE FATHER'S ROLE

Children who are deprived of a masculine paternal presence are more likely to become defensive and rigidly adhere to cultural role standards or to avoid the behavior expected of their gender. One study of paternally deprived boys on projective tests and interviews with their mothers indicated that father separation was associated with compensatory masculinity—the boys at times behaving in an exaggerated masculine manner, at other times behaving in a highly feminine manner. The father-separated boys seemed much less secure in their masculinity.[6]

It should not be implied from this, however, that masculinity is founded on an image of male dominance. While sons look to identify with a powerful paternal figure, research shows that if the father is controlling, restrictive, and punishing, the boy is low in masculinity.[7] Extreme paternal dominance squelches the development of independence and competence in the child, two of the hallmarks of traditional masculinity.

For instance, Jim, whom I wrote about in the previous chapter, had developed a "Hemingway" type of masculine persona to compensate for an underlying masculine insecurity. Jim's relationship to his alcoholic father is illustrative of how father domination can stifle the development of a secure masculine persona as much as can an absent father or domination by a mother. In Jim's case, rather than avoiding the characteristics of the traditional masculine role, as did Jake, he manifested them in a defensive manner. Jim had not really developed and integrated those qualities, he merely acted them in an exaggerated style.

To really develop the traditional masculine role, the young boy needs an environment that encourages exploration. The boy needs to be able to try out different behaviors and feelings, practice and display them, and have an audience—especially a male audience—that mirrors back how wonderful and masculine he is. Such a situation allows the masculine characteristics to develop into a comfortable and integrated part of the adult personality. If the young boy's attempts at being masculine are met by a lack of mirroring or, even worse, derision and abuse by the father, as was the case with Jim, his willingness to explore, develop, and display becomes limited. He is not ashamed of the masculine role itself, only of his ability to manifest it competently. Since he feels his own incompetence, one defensive alternative is to compensate and exaggerate for appearance' sake what is not truly developed and a part of himself.

It is clear, in conclusion, that the role of the father is critical in the development of the son's masculine gender role. The experience of the father as fearsome and threatening is not the normal experience that boys have of their fathers, as was once thought, nor is it the basis for developing a masculine gender role. In fact, when the father is frightening and excessively dominant to the son, an exaggerated masculine persona often results. In these instances the male has an insecure masculine development based on the defense mechanism of identification with the aggressor.

On the other hand, when a boy has a loving relationship with a masculine, competent, and nurturing father, he develops the masculine characteristics of his father, and insofar as the father is representative of his culture, the boy develops the behavior and attitudes appropriate for a male. He identifies with the traditional masculinity and feels good about his maleness. It is only from this position of masculine security that he can later open himself to the possibility of becoming a male human being, a person able to experience and integrate characteristics common to all human beings, not only traditional to men.

THE ISAAC COMPLEX

Identification with the father, while necessary and positive for the development of the masculine role and, ultimately, for becoming a male human being, can also lead to the typical problem of overidentification with the masculine values of the culture.

In mythology, the hero's fight with the Great Mother is symbolic of the individual's struggle to break free of various identifications, the first of which is with the personal mother. For the development of individuality, however, a person needs to do more than separate from the mother. A heroic fight with the father must also take place.

The father is often symbolic of the old order and the young hero is representative of the new. Fathers represent and reinforce the religious, ethical, political, and social values of the collective. The outer father and the inner father image are conditioned by the character of the culture transmitting these values. As noted earlier, research shows that fathers exert a greater effect than mothers on the formation of gender roles for both sons and daughters. Mothers tend to treat their children the same, without regard to whether the child is male or female. Fathers, on the other hand, in their concern for society's standards, tend to reinforce the instrumental/active dimension in boys and the expressive/passive dimension in girls.

The danger from the father is that he may fix consciousness in the wrong direction by upholding the old system of values. Fathers impress the values of their generation on the young; the young who identify with them are included among the adults. While this identification with the father mitigates the power of the unconscious identification with the mother, the mother identification is replaced by an unconscious identification with traditional collective masculine values. There results a stable sameness between culture, parent, and child that is devoid of generational conflict. People who are completely identified with convention and collective norms by means of identification with the father are psychologically castrated—they cannot develop into full human beings who move beyond the limitations of the traditional culture. They merely live out what is because it always has been. I'll give two examples, in terms of male psychology, of psychological castration due to patriarchal overidentification.

In the Old Testament book of Genesis the story is told of Abraham and Isaac. Abraham was an old man, one hundred years old at the time, when his wife, Sarah, became pregnant with Isaac. Abraham loved this child of his old age. God decided to test Abraham's faith and ordered Abraham to sacrifice Isaac. Abraham went to the mountain as God had directed him, built an altar, piled it high with firewood, and tied Isaac to the top. As he reached for the knife to plunge into his son, God intervened and told Abraham to stop, he had proven his fear of God. Then a ram appeared caught in a bush, and Abraham sacrificed the ram in place of his son. As a result of this proof of his obedience to God, Abraham was promised that his descendants would be a mighty people.

This story is usually told to provide an example of Abraham's faith in God. I like to think of the story from the point of view of Isaac, as an example of how a son's individuality is castrated by a developmental overidentification with his father. Isaac shows complete and utter reliance on his father. After all, God did not order Isaac to kill himself. The order was to Abraham. Thus Isaac was subject to his father's relationship to God and his father's spiritual values, not his own.

Isaac's position is in many ways quite natural. It is normal for a son to want to be like his father; he feels proud when he can identify with him adequately enough to be accepted by other adult males as a man who is like his father. The benefits of such developmental identification with the father are the transmission of the cultural values of the collective, acceptance by the collective, a secure masculine identity, and being in-cluded among the adults. An inability to identify successfully brings feelings of inferiority, shame, and betrayal.

A contemporary example of Isaac's relationship to his fa-ther—an Isaac complex, if you will—comes from a colleague who told me that one of the things that made him proud as an adolescent was working with his father, a peasant immigrant from Russia, on his furniture-moving truck. They worked six-teen hours a day, six days a week. No matter how exhausted they were, no matter how much their bodies hurt, no one ever complained. He remembered how great it felt as a boy to be a man like his father. Only years later did he realize that he had been initiated into the masculinity of a Russian peasant. He remained unconsciously identified with that collective peasant identity of physical toil until his early thirties, when he went to live in a wood-heated house in the mountains and spent untold hours cutting and chopping firewood. He realized then, with a great sense of betraying his father, that he hated being like that. He really was not meant to be a beast of burden. He valued consciousness and psychological development, not the activity-based masculinity of his father.

Another example of the Isaac Complex is Frank, a tremendous athlete I once knew. He played baseball so superbly that he was offered a contract to play in the farm system of the New York Mets. Frank idealized his father, who was a carpenter. He asked his father whether or not to take the offer by the Mets. The father told Frank that there was an opening in the carpenter's union, a rare event, and that he could get his son the slot. He advised his son to take the secure union job, rather than risk the uncertainty of a baseball career.

Frank followed his father's suggestion. Years later I asked him—now thirty years old, married with children, and playing ball for barroom teams—why he had made the decision he made and how he now felt about it. Frank said his decision was based on love of his father; his father was his idol, and Frank wanted to be just like him. Besides, to do otherwise would have been a betrayal, a statement that his father's way was not good enough for the son. Continuing his father's life had been Frank's way of not rejecting his father and thereby avoiding the guilt of betrayal. Yet Frank said he was no longer sure he had made the right decision.

The second example of psychological castration, a reaction to the Isaac Complex, is the permanent revolutionary. While this type of man appears to be a hero who is always struggling to free himself from authority and tradition, he is really a false hero. He rebels against authority simply because authority is associated with his father, not because he has come to an individual position of his own. Such a person can never assume power himself, never be a father. He is tied to the old values by always having to rebel against them. He cannot come to a true position of his own.

For example, Carl, an analysand, swore as an adolescent that he would never grow up to be a man like his father, a powerful, cold, and violent businessman. Carl rebelled by remaining an irresponsible adolescent, what he considered the opposite of his father. Carl never kept a schedule, so he always came late for appointments; he never organized his financial affairs, so his bills were never paid on time or his checks bounced. To avoid being an adult husband Carl carried on clandestine affairs; to avoid being a grown-up father he ignored his child; to avoid being an adult provider Carl sabotaged one job opportunity after another. Through all this Carl had the satisfaction of saying he was not a man like his father. Since all he was doing was rebelling, however, Carl never bothered to develop himself into any kind of adult male; instead, he remained an adolescent. When Carl and his family first moved from the city to the suburbs and the neighborhood adolescents addressed Carl as "Mister," Carl could not at first understand that they were speaking to him. In his mind, after all, he was an adolescent just like them, not a "Mister"!

In remaining an adolescent rebellious to his father, Carl was psychologically castrated; he could not develop into an adult, much less move beyond the traditional masculine role to becoming a male human being. Carl's castrated state was exemplified by his explanation of the passive way he had presented himself at a job interview: he had not wanted to appear too "cocky." Symbolically, Carl was saying that he did not want anyone to experience him as having too much "cock," that is, as having an adult penis. For the first time, Carl understood the implication of his choice of words and realized that, for him, having "cock" meant that he was an adult male; psychological castration was the price he had been paying for his rebellion.

These examples of the Isaac complex are all illustrative of men who sacrificed their individuality either to rebel against their fathers or to avoid feelings of betrayal and guilt for being different than their fathers. Fear of deviance, with its attendant feelings of inadequacy and shame, is another obstacle that prevents men from defining their masculinity in a way that differs from that of the father and the masculine collective.

Fear of deviance is a fear of engaging in behavior that contradicts culturally learned role behavior and thereby threatens gender role standards. Fear of deviance is based on realistic experiences about the negative consequences of deviating from norms. The actual consequences of deviance can account for that fear and result in an urge toward conformity. Fear of deviance causes men to avoid certain goals—emotional and psychological development, for example—that they consider unmasculine.

Some men who recognize the limitations of the narrow masculine role in which they have been raised worry that if they give up that role women will reject them as deviant. While their anxiety is often due to the projection of their own fears onto women, in many instances it is an accurate perception of conflicts women have about men. Despite protestations to the contrary, many women are conflicted about their desire to relate to nontraditional men. On the one hand, these women desire a man who is open, sensitive, related, and egalitarian. On the other hand, due to their own father identifications, they want a man who embodies the traditional masculine values of strength, independence, and invulnerability.

One woman I worked with in psychotherapy provides an example of how such a conflict affects both men and women. This woman had married a man who, like her traditionally masculine father, was cold in his feelings, withdrawn, and did not believe in displaying feelings of weakness. She was troubled by her husband's unwillingness to share his inner anxieties and conflicts with her. As a result of his own psychotherapy, the man slowly began to change. He recognized his own insecurity and vulnerability and began to speak to his wife about these parts of himself. Was she happy? Yes, on the surface. But she had a way of making hurtful comments to her husband every time he revealed himself. When he complained to her about this she declared him to be oversensitive and defensive, further alienating him and forcing him back into his withdrawn, cold, unfeeling position.

Meanwhile, the woman's dreams revealed that she was conflicted about her husband's change. Her husband's insecurities aroused dependency conflicts that lay hidden behind the traditional roles she and her husband lived. If her husband was weak, then she would have to assume more responsibility and let him lean on her.

On one level, this woman wanted to be stronger and more independent; on another, she took comfort in her traditional feminine position of passivity and having a "strong" man around to take care of her. Also, she unconsciously identified with her father. While she had adopted an egalitarian rhetoric, she really believed that masculinity, which she defined in terms of her father's silent, strong, and controlling behavior, was superior. Femininity she considered weak and submissive. When her husband revealed his fears he, in her mind, became a weak, inferior woman. She, in turn, became the superior, aggressive male and derived great unconscious satisfaction from her subtle sadistic comments.

Another example of a man afraid of deviance was Stan, another analysand, who refused to show any feelings except anger to his family or friends. His wife was threatening to leave the marriage because of the emotional shallowness in the relationship. Coming to therapy was a last, shameful, and desperate attempt on Stan's part to change. Yet he could no more discuss his feelings with me than with others.

During the third month of therapy Stan had an anxiety attack in the waiting room before his session. He thought of walking out and leaving a note saying he would never return. Instead, he waited and started the session in his usual hostile manner, criticizing my attire and professional competence. Finally, as he began to discuss the frightening experience he had had in the waiting room, he realized that he had begun to trust and like me over the last few months. This aroused the danger of needing me, feeling dependent and showing feelings.

"Why should that frighten you?" I asked.

Stan got red in the face and his voice started to tremble. "I might cry," he said, "and you would make fun of me."

Stan then told of painful experiences in his childhood when his father and older brother teased him unmercifully with names like "sissy" and "fairy" for crying. Real men, they said, controlled themselves and did not act weak. Stan naturally identified with their masculine viewpoint and developed a hatred of his own sensitive, emotional nature. Any behavior that was not stereotypically masculine became feminine. Rather than study art, he chose his father's "more masculine" craft of plumbing.

As he grew older his fears of not being masculine elaborated into a fear of homosexuality. In his therapy he was terrified of two things. The first was that if he showed his feelings I would consider him gay and humiliate and reject him. The second and even more frightening fear was that I was really homosexual and was trying to seduce him. With great shame he told me that he had often wondered about my sexuality. I seemed to be a warm, feeling type of person who encouraged the expression of his feelings and did not respond to his viselike handshake by increasing the pressure of my own. These were behaviors that, if he did them himself, would cause him to feel nonmasculine.

In mythology, the true hero fights the father to attain his own individuality, not as a mere reaction. A man follows an "inner voice" that tells him there is a new way to live. It is because he listens to this inner voice and wants the world to change that he becomes a breaker of the old law and an enemy of the ruling system and thus comes into conflict with the "fathers" and their spokesman, the personal father. The "inner voice" a man listen to is his own urge toward individual development. His consciousness is expanded by a new idea, a new conception of how things can be, and he, as the hero, has the courage to follow that understanding. As soon as he listens to himself, as soon as he honors his individuality, he is psychologically in conflict with the father world. This is a struggle we all must go through in our personal development. To fail to separate from the father means to live a limited life as far as the development of individuality is concerned.

A DEFENSIVE IDEALIZATION OF THE FATHER

Admiration occurs when we recognize and value qualities in others that we may not have ourselves. Idealization, in contrast, indicates something extreme and unreal. In this case, our perceptions of the other are exaggerated, and we may even ascribe to the other the coveted qualities of happiness, power, goodness, and omnipotence.

Jung, like many psychoanalytic writers, recognized that idealization has both normal and defensive aspects.[8] He acknowledged that, as a normal developmental phenomenon, the first objects of idealization were the parents, whom the child fantasizes as omnipotent.

Jung differed from the other psychoanalytic writers, however, in that they viewed the idealized parental images as made up of the actual, though exaggerated, qualities of the real parents. Jung, on the other hand, found the source of the idealization not in the personal experiences of childhood but in the projection of archetypes.

For Jung, the parents are the recipients of archetypal projections from the child; these projections give the parents their omnipotent qualities. He says that these images "outweigh the influence of sensory stimuli and mold them into conformity with a preexisting psychic image."[9] It is the numinosity of the archetypes that supplies the exaggerated qualities, not the actuality of the parents. A mother, for instance, becomes an all-good, bountiful mother primarily because the nourishing aspect of the Great Mother is projected, not because the personal mother's nourishing qualities are exaggerated. Similarly, behind the personal father stands the Father archetype, which endows the personal figure with its fascination and helps explain the secret of the father's power.

Idealized figures are primary objects of identification; we try to be like those we idealize. As the first object of idealization, the mother provides the source of many of our earliest identifications. In terms of the development of the masculine gender role, the father provides the child with an other-than-mother ideal with which to identify. The idealized father provides his son with an adored model he can identify with to fill out the image of the masculine that has been split from the feminine. Since the son is developmentally meant to split masculine and feminine into opposites and develop his masculine gender role prior to, and as a prerequisite for, becoming a male human being, the paternal numinosity serves the purpose of attracting the son along this teleological path.

If development proceeds normally, according to Jung, there occurs an increasing discrimination between the real figures of the parents and the archetypal forms. The archetypal images, and the energy associated with them, fall into the unconscious of the growing personality and are available for future projection. Idealizing feelings are slowly replaced by more realistic perceptions. The son's masculinity is increasingly freed from identity with the father, and the son can then integrate aspects of the totality not limited by the father's gender role. By the end of adolescence, when development proceeds normally, the son is able to see his father neither as an ideal figure to be replicated nor as the disappointing fallen idol, but as a man in his own right.

I remember an experience with my son that illustrates the process of withdrawing idealizing energy from the father. Jesse was about eleven years old when he and I were having dinner in a restaurant. I ordered a plain yogurt, something Jesse had always eaten too. This time, however, he ordered a cherry-flavored yogurt. I asked him why the change?

Jesse responded, "I hate plain yogurt."

Surprisingly hurt, yet curious, I asked, "But why did you always order it before?"

"Because you always ate plain yogurt," Jesse responded. "You were my idol and I wanted to be just like you. But I never really liked plain yogurt, the taste is too sour."

That little interchange illustrates the son's idealization of the father, the pleasure they both receive from the idealization, and the son's realization of his individuality. Jesse really did not like the taste of plain yogurt and was ready to acknowledge his own tastes as a male separate from those of his father. In turn, I, as his father, had to accept the loss of that bit of idealizing identification from my son; I could feel a sadness about letting him go and losing the mirror that his attempt to replicate me provided. At the same time, amid the complexity of feelings this incident provoked, I could also feel pride in the development of my son's individuality and excitement over the prospect of discovering his true nature as he discovered it himself.

When the withdrawal of idealization does not occur, and for defensive reasons the earliest forms of idealization continue past their age-appropriate phase, idealization interferes with individual development. An inappropriate fascination with the father as an ideal remains, and the son's efforts go into an attempt to more fully identify with the father regardless of whether the son's individuality is in accord with the father's psychology. An identification based on the son's age-inappropriate idealization of the father results in an alienating loss of masculine individuality; a feeling of masculine inadequacy is the result of failure to identify.

The reasons for defensive idealizations are many.[10] A fear of masculine inadequacy is commonly due to an underlying identification with the mother. The basis for such a defensive idealization is strengthened when the son is constitutionally more similar to the mother than to the father and the son grows up in a patriarchal family structure that devalues the feminine. An example of such a situation is the story of Bob.

AN EXAMPLE: BOB

Bob's presenting symptom was a debilitating envy coupled with feelings of masculine inadequacy and spiritual emptiness. In discussing his symptoms, Bob realized that they were related to competitiveness with his older brother, Jack, whom Bob experienced as more adequate as a man. Jack was socially secure, with many male and female friends. He was handsome, with broad shoulders. He was financially successful. By contrast, Bob was small, thin shouldered, shy, socially insecure, and financially unsuccessful. He had followed his spiritual inclinations and become a minister, a choice that had left him relatively poor and, worst of all, spiritually unfulfilled.

As the years went by, the particular things for which Bob envied Jack changed, but the envy remained and generalized to others, so that Bob came to envy all men who had anything he did not have. Bob felt they were more adequate as men because they had what he desired. Not only did Bob covet what other men had, but in the depths of his envious rage he wished that they would feel inadequate and inferior about themselves and envy him. It did not matter whether Bob loved the other person; it just bothered him when something good happened to them and pleased him if misfortune befell them. Bob was ashamed of these feelings, considering them a base aspect of himself.

A number of months after his therapy began, Bob came to his session in an agitated state. The evening prior he had had dinner with Jack, who while talking about his many affairs with women other than his wife, had said, "The apple does not fall far from the tree." When Bob had asked him what he meant, Jack had replied quite proudly that their father had also had numerous affairs and that he was just like him. Bob had been filled with feelings of inferiority. He then reported the following dream:

> I'm outside the door of an apartment in a house in Brooklyn. I'm delivering milk with Dad, like we used to do when

I worked with him as a teenager. Seems I'm to be moving
into the apartment. Somebody opens the door from our
side and says the previous tenant has already moved and
left his stuff. Dad and I go in and look at the furniture
and other possessions to see if anything of value is there.
We make jokes about finding money or other valuables. It's
a one-bedroom apartment, which I'll be living in by myself.
I awoke from the dream thinking of women I'd like to
have affairs with.

In associating to the dream, Bob said the apartment felt like
the kind of working-class walk-up that his father would live in.
Bob would not live in such a place; it was in the wrong kind
of neighborhood and it would not be large enough for his
family.

I commented to Bob that if he lived in such an apartment
he would be able to fulfill his desire to be like his idealized
father, the figure that lay behind the envy of his brother. In this
apartment Bob too could have affairs, then he could be as adequate as Jack, the proud carbon copy of their father.

Since the apartment was too small for his family, I wondered
what the dream said about his marital relationship, and that of
his father and Jack.

Bob said that as he drove home from his dinner with Jack
he had fantasies of an affair with a woman in his congregation.
At home, when his wife tried to relate to him, Bob felt completely distant from her, angry at her for interrupting his fantasized relationship with his congregant.

"I guess I did what Dad and Jack do," Bob said. "I went off
with another woman and found my wife uninteresting to be
with."

Bob said that both his father and brother were uninterested
in their wives or in deepening their marital relationships. They

had traditional marriages of a functional kind in which the men kept emotional distance from their wives. Jack and his father never shared what was going on inside them and showed no interest in the inner lives of their spouses.

Bob said that whenever he felt intimate and vulnerable with his wife he was ravaged by feelings of masculine inferiority. He would then recover his feelings of masculine adequacy by becoming critical and angry with his wife, feeling dissatisfied sexually, and thinking that he had a right to more than one woman, as Jack and his father did.

Over the next few months, Bob's dreams and our discussions clarified the inner attack on his masculinity that he felt whenever he was intimate with his wife. Bob realized that as a man he was ashamed of the pleasure he received from loving his wife and his desire for a deep sharing of their inner lives.

"A real man is a player," Bob declared. "That's what Jack keeps telling me. He's like Dad, powerful and in control. He's happy. I'm a wimp. All I want to do is love my wife."

A number of weeks later Bob dreamed: "I am trying to convince my brother and father that we still have things in common. My brother emphasizes repeatedly that we have nothing in common. I cry and fight against accepting this."

This dream was very important to Bob. He quoted from memory a passage from the Gospel According to Saint Matthew where Jesus says: "Do not suppose that I have come to bring peace to the earth: it is not peace I have come to bring, but a sword. For I have come to set a man against his father, a daughter against her mother, a daughter-in-law against her mother-in-law. A man's enemies will be those of his own household" (Matthew 10:34–36). Bob had often wondered about Jesus' statement of setting the son against his father and the daughter against her mother.

I agreed with Bob's sword analogy and offered as an amplification the alchemical process of *separatio*. In this procedure a component is differentiated out of a mixture. Psychologically, the goal of such a process of differentiation is to create duality so that the component can be brought to consciousness. Consciousness develops as a consequence of opposition brought about by differentiation and the subsequent resolution of the conflict. Only that which is separated can unite.

In Bob's dream, a conscious conflict was being set up between himself and the traditional masculine values represented by his brother and father. The unconscious was trying to force Bob to undergo a necessary step in the transformative process that leads to wholeness. But the initial consequence of such a separation from unconscious containment in family identification is sadness and mourning.

Shortly after this discussion Bob dreamed: "It's nighttime in Brooklyn. I'm driving with Jack next to me in a small open car, like a golf cart. I take a side trip to Nostrand Avenue. A skunk is coming toward us. I turn off the lights and tell Jack not to move, hoping the skunk will just pass us by. Instead, the skunk sprays us."

In his associations to this dream, Bob said that when the family lived on Nostrand Avenue their father spent all his free time in their garage fixing milk boxes and that their mother would be upset over being ignored. It was when they lived on Nostrand Avenue that Jack first started working with their father on his milk truck and learned about their father's having sex with other women. The skunk Bob associated with immoral behavior, as in the expression "He's a skunk."

As for the image of turning off the car's lights, Bob commented that it was a way of hiding from the skunk. He hoped, in the dream, that it would make it impossible to be seen. He now also realized that without lights it would be difficult to see. In that sense, the dream image was a picture of someone trying to be unconscious.

From our discussion of the dream, Bob and I concluded that Bob was trying to be unconscious of how both he and Jack were contaminated by their father's immorality. Rather than idealizing him, something in Bob disapproved of his father's behavior and values.

Bob then recalled the *separatio* symbolism from his previous dream. He realized that one of the things that differentiated him from his father and Jack was his moral reaction. Bob felt that it was wrong for them to cheat and lie to their wives; if his brother and father wanted to have affairs they should have the courage to be honest about it.

To further this differentiation I suggested another point of view, that the affairs of Jack and his father were a sign of unhappiness in their marriages. Both men were married to women they had to hide from and from whom they could get no love and support.

One of the differences between Jack and him, Bob continued, was that Jack was proud of his similarity to their father. Jack had succeeded in identifying with their father. Bob, on the other hand, was ambivalent. When he let himself be conscious of who his father and brother were, he realized he considered them immoral. The conflict, however, was that Bob also felt inadequate as a man because he was not successfully identified with his father, at least not in the realm of having affairs, keeping secrets from his wife, and being unrelated to his feelings.

"I'm sensitive, shy, socially insecure, and faithful," Bob declared. "I have feelings. I care about spiritual values. This is more like my Mom, not Dad. I'm like my mother in many ways, and Jack is like Dad. But I'm ashamed to be like Mother,

so that leaves being like Father, which Jack is. So I'm inadequate as a man, envious of Jack."

Bob's conflict over his similarity to his mother was important to his development as an individual. His slow acceptance
of her qualities as a significant part of his personality helped
end his defensive idealization of his father's limited masculinity. Bob was able to reflect more consciously on his father,
realizing that his father had traditional masculine qualities that
he legitimately admired, such as an ability to work hard and
support his family, but that he also had many qualities that
Bob considered primitive and immoral.

Rather than continuing to idealize his brother's happy identification with their father, Bob realized that he wanted to live
his life in a more individual manner. Bob announced this realization one day when he came to his session and said: "Jack
always says that 'the apple doesn't fall far from the tree.' Today
I realized that is only partly true. The apple also shouldn't fall
too close to the tree."

The issue slowly ceased to be whether Bob or Jack was better off, but that they were different and that Bob had idealized
Jack for unconscious reasons. While Bob could recognize qualities in Jack that he could admire and respect, areas where Jack
was objectively more developed than himself, he realized he
would not trade places with his brother, whom he considered
emotionally and intellectually shallow.

The underlying conflict that men have over identification
with the feminine is not unique to Bob, and it is extremely
significant for men in general.[11] Earlier in this chapter we saw
it in the example of Stan, who feared that his sensitive feelings
would be misunderstood as a humiliating sign of femininity.
The fear of feminine identification is also evident in the ho-
mophobia rampant in American society. In a subsequent chap-

ter, we will discuss the conflicts aroused in men owing to their lifelong identification with mother.

For now it is important to consider another consequence of Bob's idealization of his father and brother, the loss of his spiritual values.

Common for men in our society is the association between external accomplishment and wealth, both characteristic of the traditional masculine role. Less commonly understood is the symbolic relationship between wealth and spiritual wisdom. In alchemy, for instance, the alchemists attempted to turn base material, such as lead, into gold. Jung understood that the alchemists were in actuality projecting a psychological process onto the material world: "Alchemy was not concerned with ordinary goldmaking but with a philosophical secret. For these alchemists the gold undoubtedly had a symbolic nature."[12] The attempt to transform a base substance was in actuality symbolic of psychological transformation. Jung concluded that in their search for spiritual and philosophical wisdom, the alchemists often confused the material with the spiritual.

During the period when Bob was discussing his envy of his brother's wealth and self-confidence he reported the following dream: "Jack is in the showroom attached to the front of one of his factories. He is selling some coats to two female buyers. At first they are not going to buy his products, but are going to buy from a competitor who is cheaper. Jack is dazzling in his salesmanship, pointing out the finer points of his coats, leaning over confidently and touching one of the women on the arm for emphasis. Jack is dressed elegantly, shaved perfectly, and he points his gold pen for emphasis. The women are convinced and purchase his coats."

In discussing the dream, Bob said that what most impressed him was Jack's manner. Jack seemed completely relaxed and self-assured, seemingly without anxiety, insecurity, or inferiority feelings. What gave Jack this inner security, Bob continued, was his material success. Jack had fulfilled their father's ideal and acquired the great wealth that made a man successful as a man, and now he could rest confidently inside himself.

Especially interesting for Bob was his observation that the inner security and self-confidence that Jack manifested in the dream was what Bob had always expected he would himself feel as a result of finding spiritual meaning. Bob began to realize that his identification with the values of his father and Jack had lead to the adoption of their idea that material gain ultimately brings inner security and personal value. The reason Bob had originally chosen the ministry as his vocation was because he deeply believed that his only hope for true inner peace and security was a life imbued with spiritual meaning; he knew that mere material questing was destined to leave him spiritually empty. Yet his idealized image of his brother had Jack attaining the personal security that comes from the spiritual meaning that Bob himself craved.

I commented that this did not make sense. Jack's need to brag about his affairs and his overidentification with their father all indicated underlying insecurity and inferiority feelings. I wondered what about Jack's material success Bob imagined as actually giving Jack such confidence. I suggested to Bob that he fantasize that he had all his brother's money and paternal approval. Did he feel secure and adequate?

Bob responded that he still felt dissatisfied and envious. There was something projected onto his brother that remained after Bob took Jack's money. In the fantasy, what Jack still had was "satisfaction," an inner peace and security that came from a deep understanding about the nature of existence. Bob knew this to be untrue in reality. Jack was a driven businessman, almost single-mindedly devoted to the accumulation of wealth and power, and did not care one whit for inner peace and spiritual meaning.

I then suggested that Bob change the fantasy and leave Jack with his wealth and instead take his spiritual wisdom.

This made a big difference for Bob. It was not really the money that was important. Even if Bob remained in his current financial condition, the acquisition of the spiritual understanding that Bob projected onto Jack's money brought Bob an increase in his own inner peace and a decrease in his own feelings of dissatisfaction and envy.

After much reflection Bob said, "I think I've confused inferiority with lack of money and spiritual wisdom with material gain and masculinity. I've been projecting my urge for spiritual accomplishment onto the symbol of my brother's money as a literal drive for gold rather than for the gold of spiritual wisdom."

Conclusions

At first it was thought that fathers did not play a significant role in the development of their children. Subsequent research has contradicted those initial impressions. One study goes so far as to suggest that the little boy is biologically programmed by androgenization of the fetal brain to turn away from the mother and toward the father.[13] Its author says that the development of core gender identity can be impaired if the male child lacks a male parent at the critical juncture when gender identity is consolidated. Other evidence suggests that separation from the father prior to four years of age impairs the development of the son's masculine gender role.[14]

For the boy to feel adequate as a male he must develop

competency in the traditional characteristics of the masculine gender role—the instrumental/active dimension. Imitation and identification with the father is how the boy seeks his masculine gender role. An absent, weak, or passive father, domination of the father and the son by the mother, or domination and abuse of the son by the father can lead to pathological forms of masculine development. For instance, an abusive father can cause a son to fear to explore and integrate the various characteristics of the masculine gender role. The result is often an exaggerated caricature of that role, which serves to compensate for an underlying insecurity. Rather than assertion, aggression and domination result; rather than ambition for satisfaction in creative work, workaholism and a quest for hierarchical power consumes the individual; rather than the desire for competence, the need for perfection takes over.

On the other hand, a nurturing, affectionate father who is perceived as powerful and valuable can lead the boy to a developmental identification with the father. The father provides the boy with the model he seeks, and the son wants to be like the father he loves and admires. The boy identifies with the father and explores the various attributes the father manifests. A secure traditional masculine gender role develops.

While the development of a secure traditional gender role is necessary for the male, the identification with the father and the traditional culture can also be limiting. Out of the security of the traditional, individuality must develop. After a man has successfully identified with his father's masculine role, he must then begin the process of separating his personality from that of his father's way of being masculine. Fear of deviance, feelings of betrayal and guilt, and the difficulty of withdrawing idealization from the father are all impediments that the man must struggle with in separating from the father and the traditional masculine culture.

In becoming more individual, a man does not give up the masculine characteristics he has acquired. It is the father's attitude toward them and the father's way of actualizing the traditionally masculine that changes. The individual male retains the characteristics of the instrumental/active dimension; they are universal characteristics necessary for wholeness, essential to being a male human being who can live an effective and competent life.

For instance, a boy may have acquired the qualities of assertion and competition through an identification with a father who is a wealthy businessman. The son may ultimately decide to use these characteristics consciously in a way similar to his father's, or he may decide to use them not to acquire wealth but to fight for the environment, competing with polluting companies for political power. It is the ability to be assertive and competitive that he must retain from his identification with his father; the attitude and the manifestation need to become individual. What is required at this stage in the process of becoming a male human being is an individual attitude toward the instrumental/active characteristics, and a conscious way to live them.

5 | Masculinity and Achievement Conflicts
The Shadow Speaks

Men consider external achievement to be one of the more significant characteristics of the male gender role. They aspire to attain higher status, and they are perceived by themselves and others as more masculine when they succeed. Lack of achievement, on the other hand, leads men to be considered failures and, even worse, feminine. In one study, for example, subjects were presented with short verbal cues in which male or female characters succeeded or failed at a range of male- and female-dominated occupations. The subjects then rated the characters on adjective scales on the basis of what they thought the person might be like. Results showed that males who failed were rated by the subjects as less powerful and more feminine than those who succeeded regardless of whether they failed at a profession dominated by either males or females.[1]

When people of either sex succeed or fail at a task they typically attribute their success or failure to some cause—their ability, effort, luck, or the difficulty of the task. Which cause is attributed in a particular circumstance is a result of such factors as gender stereotypes and neurotic pressures. It is common to attribute a man's successes to effort and ability and his failures to bad luck or the difficulty of the task. The converse holds true for women. Neurosis leads to another kind of causal attribution. A fear of successful achievement creates anxiety, which may cause men and women to choose to deny that an achievement was due to their efforts or ability; luck is a more common explanation.

There are three patterns of causal attribution. First, a man might logically appraise the situation so that his failure or success is rationally attributed to objective factors based on available information. Second, he might take a defensive or self-enhancing tack, attributing his failures to external factors and successes to internal factors. Such a cognitive bias allows one to include favorable information and exclude unfavorable information from one's self-image. Third, he might adopt a self-derogatory bias, attributing success to external causes and failure to internal causes.[2]

Success and failure are so significant to the masculine self-image that men resort more frequently than women to biased and defensive attributions as explanation. For example, in one study subjects competed in an anagram test that was prearranged in level of difficulty so that one subject would clearly defeat a partner. Afterward the subjects were asked to attribute their own performances to some degree of skill or luck. The major finding of the study was that males were more likely to attribute their successes to skill, an internal cause, and their failures to luck, an external cause. Females, on the other hand, who in our society are generally less involved with winning and high achievement, tended to attribute both their successes and their failures to relatively equal proportions of skill.[3]

Equating masculinity with external accomplishment, and external accomplishment with financial success and power, exerts an unfortunate and insidious social pressure on the self-esteem of many men. Such an equation inhibits men from formulating individual values distinct from those of the dominant society. Men who value internal achievements, devotion to family, and commitment to society, none of which may lead to external recognition, wealth, or power, face the danger of denigration. For example, some men may have their own reasons for refusing promotions that carry increased prestige, money, and power; other men may want to reject materialistic and competitive goals, even if they are defined as more socially successful. Often men realize that many outcomes defined by the culture as success also carry negative qualities. A higher position in a company, for instance, might necessitate moving to another city and away from satisfying friendships, a good school, and nearby family. Or the position might necessitate working nights and thus spending less time with one's spouse and children. It is not always easy, however, for men to reject such seemingly positive situations when the alternative is diminishment in the eyes of the masculine collective.

To the observer steeped in the values of the culture, it is often difficult to discern whether a man is suffering from some conflict over achievement or whether he is functioning on something deeper than a level of identification with collective goals; he may in fact be achieving the fulfillment of consciously held individual values. Some men are capable of recognizing that their destiny is not to be what they have been collectively conditioned to be. They understand that to be truly an individual a person must be able to recognize and apply his energy toward fulfillment in the direction they are meant to develop. Such men reach the point of separation from the collective where they are capable of reexamining the outer goals with which they have identified their masculinity—whether for fame, position, wealth, or something else—and altering them to the needs of the total person.

Men who are freed from collective identifications are free to experience their genuine selves and to choose activities that express their individuality rather than collective masculine norms.

Inner experiences and outer activities are then sensed to be representative of their very nature. Even everyday activities may take on the quality of a religious experience, and one's own self is then experienced as a vessel through which manifest one's true creative energies. Only through such experiences can life be imbued with meaning.

ACHIEVEMENT ANXIETY

Competition pits human against human and, in its best form, may incite an individual to function at his highest capacity or make an extra effort to achieve a goal. But competition has gone too far in our society, especially in the quest for external achievement. Many men compete in order to win, not for the pleasure of being fully engaged in an activity that represents their true self. Unchecked, competition for external goals may result in racism, sexism, and colonialism, as well as the rape of the natural environment in the pursuit of economic power. Aggression, unmediated by relatedness, can lead to cruelty and war. Exaggerated independence may inhibit society's ability to solve common problems by failing to recognize the fundamental interdependence among humans and between humankind and the physical environment. Rationality, when applied excessively and solely in the pursuit of competitive advantage, can result in a technological and scientific system incapable of recognizing and granting legitimacy to human needs and feelings.

Despite the overemphasis on external success in our society, the ability to focus one's energies in the pursuit of constructive accomplishment is important. Even if a man's goals are a true representation of his individual nature, his success in the external world requires the ability to be decisive and competitive and to control the use of assertion and aggression, qualities traditionally associated with the masculine gender role. Anything that interferes with the development of these qualities in men will also impede their ability to achieve such success.

For females in our society, conflicts over external achievement are based as often on societal pressures to conform to gender roles as on neurotic conflict. The situation for men is different. Since achievement is such a socially sanctioned aspect of their gender role, fear of achievement in men is much more commonly due to neurotic conflict.

My experience indicates that two criteria are necessary for serious anxiety over achievement to develop in males. First, the young boy's normal fears have to be intensified by environmental circumstances, and secondly, his natural motivation to develop has to meet with interference from a parent or someone acting in the role of a parent.

A parent's anxiety as a young boy appears to be developing, separating, and gaining skills and independence can exacerbate the child's normal fears. Because this process begins when the boy is very young, often before the boy can recognize that his feelings are separate from those of the parent, the boy often experiences the parent's anxiety as his own. Even if the child is old enough to recognize the anxiety as belonging to his parent, the boy feels anxious as a reaction to the parent's fear. The child naturally looks for means to reduce his parent's and his own anxieties.

A boy's growth toward independence represents a threatening situation for some parents. To reduce their painful anxiety such parents may interfere with what they experience as the source of their anxiety, their son's development. Overtly, in keeping with a conscious wish that the son grow and mature, the parents may encourage his independence and striving for competence. Actual evidence of the child's success, however, arouses anxiety or anger in the parents. Parents may then subtly interfere with their son by criticizing the efforts he makes for himself, undoing what he has done and redoing it better, or becoming impatient with their son's fumbling efforts to achieve mastery. What often underlies such parental behavior is the parents' fear of their child's accomplishments.

I remember an experience with my son that gave me a sense of the conflicts that parents can go through as they experience their children's growth. When my son was three years old it was my habit when I came home from work to ask him how his day was. While I was changing my clothes he would recount his whole day's experience to me and we would psychologically merge. It was important that everything in his psyche should also be a part of my psyche. One day, as usual, I asked him about his day, and he suddenly responded, "I don't want to tell you." I felt as if my heart would break. The complete merger between us was over. I could feel myself going through a great struggle to accept this and not try to make him feel insecure so that he would feel he had to tell me.

Sometimes the parents' anxiety can be so intense that they become neurotic in the way they relate to their son's achievements; under such circumstances a serious and abiding conflict over accomplishment may be instilled in the child. A parent's difficulty with the child's growth could arise from neurotic sources of which the parent is not aware; for example, the parent's own conflicts over achievement, the parent's fear that the son will exceed his or her own achievements, or the parent's need to keep the son dependent. The particular kinds of anxiety that the parent suffers in relationship to the son's success and the particular stage in the son's development on which it impinges determine the anxieties that the child and later the adult experiences when he deals with the urge to achieve.

Neurotic fathers commonly interfere with their sons' achievements by becoming hostilely competitive with them; neurotic mothers commonly interfere by means of overt or implicit threats of abandonment. Both of these cause serious conflict in the young boy. The result is that the traditionally masculine qualities of decisiveness, competitiveness, and assertion remain undeveloped rather than developing into comfortable characteristics of the masculine gender role freely available to the ego.

The Father, Achievement, and the Son's Shadow

In discussing the persona aspect of the masculine gender role I described what a man is supposed to be like in our culture: controlled, powerful, logical, ambitious, and successful. Many human qualities are left out of this role, however. They exist as undeveloped potential in a man's unconscious. Some of these qualities are avoided because they are associated with the feminine gender role and would cause a man to feel deviant if they were an acknowledged part of his conscious life. I will discuss the effects of the dissociation of these "feminine" qualities on a man in another chapter. Other qualities are avoided, even those normally considered masculine, because of psychological conflicts.

When traditionally masculine qualities—the instrumental/active dimension—are avoided, they remain undeveloped and often appear in dreams associated with an image of another man. This image Jung called the shadow. The issue of achievement in the external world illustrates how inner conflict can inhibit the development of traditional masculine characteristics.

In the chapter on the persona I discussed the important role the father plays in the formation of the son's masculine role.

Normally the father experiences a loving desire for his son to be a man like himself, a desire the son shares out of his love and admiration for the father. Not all fathers feel comfortable with their sons' identification and attempts to replicate them, especially when the father feels competitive and is threatened by his son's development.

The Cronus myth, for example, describes a competitive father-son relationship. Uranus, jealous of his sons, thrusts them deep beneath the earth. His wife, Gaia, angry at her husband's behavior, produces a sickle of steel, which her son Cronus uses to castrate his father. Cronus, now in charge, also fears his children and swallows each at birth. Rhea, Cronus's sister and the mother of his children, deceives Cronus by substituting a rock for her youngest child, Zeus, who, when he grows to maturity, overthrows his father.

In some men such a negative relationship to a hostile and competitive father leads to a fear of failure, in others to a fear of achievement.

FEAR OF FAILURE

If left only to the pressures exerted on men by their own inner urge to develop and by a society that demands achievement from men in order to fulfill their assigned gender roles, men would fear failure and strive for success. When a man was presented with a task, his desire to achieve would spur him to effort and accomplishment. Indications of poor performance would result in even more effort. In fact, research supports the validity of these expectations. For example, in one experiment, subjects were presented with the cue "A man finds himself at the bottom (or top) of his class." The subjects were then given seventeen possible events that might follow the failure or success of the character in the cue. Results showed that a man who failed was seen as more likely to work hard in the future, to wonder if he was normal, and to worry that his girlfriend would reject him. The man at the top of his class was seen as more likely to continue to top the class, to be praised by his parents, and later to become famous in his occupation.[4]

When neurosis enters the picture the situation changes. Men who suffer from a neurotic fear of failure still want to succeed. The anxiety attendant upon failure and the need for achievement to be perfect can be so debilitating, however, that the normal effort to achieve is compromised. Such individuals prefer the status quo to the risks of achievement.

Fear of failing often prevents men from attempting to achieve their goals. An individual may feel comfortable functioning or relating at a certain level of accomplishment. If offered a higher position or an opportunity to relate to someone they consider well developed and attractive they become afraid. Such men believe that they are really inadequate and have been fooling everybody. The more demanding situation or relationship will bring to light their inadequacy and make it obvious to others. While it may appear that the man is afraid of succeeding in the new situation, in reality he is afraid of the failure that he expects to follow.

Fear of failure is associated with a history of low self-esteem, shame associated with failure, and a consequent inhibition of achievement-oriented behavior. Fear of failure is related to attitudes toward authority. Authoritarian, perfectionist, overdemanding parents who inflict on the son repeated humiliations and punishment for errors produce fear of assertive action. Men who are afraid to be wrong, who shy away from action, and who undertake everything with indecision are most comfortable with routine tasks where their proficiency is beyond question. Such individuals avoid everything new, different, and interesting. Originality, creativity, and spontaneity are most effected.

The fear of being wrong leads to perfectionism and intolerance of criticism. Every examination becomes a trial lest something wrong be discovered. Making a mistake becomes equivalent to having revealed something inferior and unacceptable. Fear of exposing their inferiorities causes some men to avoid the limelight. They shy away from any situation that might make them the center of attention.

An Example: Phil

Phil, a young law school graduate, was upset when he received an appointment as clerk to a prominent judge. While Phil was pleased by the recognition, he doubted his abilities to live up to the new responsibilities. He feared that the increased prominence would make his inevitable failure obvious to all. Phil imagined that others would gloat over his failure and take the opportunity to belittle him. The judge, in Phil's mind, would be a demanding, perfectionistic authoritarian whom Phil would never be able to satisfy and who would continually put Phil down.

Phil's relationship to his father, a powerful, successful businessman, was being reenacted in his imaginary relationship with the judge. The father, a brilliant, driven man, demanded perfection from his son. If Phil did ten things right and one wrong, the father focused on the error and severely criticized and humiliated his son. Phil developed the feeling that he could never do anything right, even when he was doing well. He developed the habit of looking at his performance as his father did and noticing what he did not do well, rather than what he did right. He then severely attacked himself.

The relationship between fear of failure, perfectionism, and masculinity was clearly manifest in one of Phil's dreams: "I'm in school taking a test. I know I've made an error and won't get the *A* I want so much. The teacher hands the test back and looks at me with clear disapproval. I've gotten a *B+*. I've failed and feel emasculated. I am filled with self-hate."

The dream indicated to Phil his equation of masculinity with success and success with perfection. In his waking life, as in the dream, Phil felt his masculinity jeopardized by any error. For Phil, the relationship between achievement and gender was solely masculine. The female gender was divorced from achievement; a woman could be either successful or not successful and still be feminine.

When others complimented him on his performance, Phil felt they had been fooled into not seeing the imperfections in his work. While he wanted and enjoyed the recognition he got from others—the recognition he had wanted but not received from his father—he also feared that the recognition would cause them to look more closely at his performance and ultimately see the flaws; then unmerciful criticism would follow. To avoid the expected criticism in his current situation, Phil needed to avoid the coveted clerkship with the judge.

During the discussion of his fears of taking the clerkship Phil dreamed:

> A man is very abusive to his adolescent son. He dominates the boy physically by pinching his cheek, and psychologically by insisting that the boy say it does not hurt. I take the boy from his father and have him move in with me. I will try to undo the damage. The father, who was separated from his passive wife, fakes a reconciliation in order to convince a judge he is a changed man. The judge sends the boy back to his family despite the obvious falseness of

the father's role. The judge is indifferent, perhaps even cruel himself. I am furious and wonder if I can sue the judge as punishment, but realize he is protected from such retribution.

The dream, by helping Phil realize that he was projecting his father onto the judge, calmed Phil's anxiety about an irrational attack on his self-esteem. Phil decided to take the clerkship, and the judge turned out not to be nearly as authoritarian as Phil had feared. The judge did like to have things done properly, however, and could be critical of those who did not meet his standards. As would be expected of any newcomer to a position, Phil made errors, and while the judge understood and encouraged Phil's development in the position, he also pointed out Phil's mistakes. Phil responded to the judge's valid criticisms as if his worth had been generally condemned. Rather than continuing to work hard, Phil became depressed, doubted his ability to handle the job, and began to give up. Naturally his performance deteriorated further. While defensively not working hard on some research the judge requested, Phil was told that his position was in jeopardy.

Phil came to his next therapy session in a panic. Another failure loomed on the horizon. After we discussed his defensive manner of relating to his fear of failure, however, Phil decided to make a great effort at his work, finished the requested research on time, and received praise for his efforts. What a difference this made. Phil's self-esteem was now buoyed and he was happy to apply himself to the judge's next request.

FEAR OF ACHIEVEMENT

As Phil's story demonstrates, men who fear failure tend to do better when told they are doing well. They do not want to fail, and encouragement inspires them to try to succeed. Their performance deteriorates when told they are doing poorly. Their feelings of inferiority and their expectations of never being able to please the perfectionist demands of the judging authorities are aroused by negative feedback.

In contrast, men who fear success react poorly to being told they do something well and after being given such recognition will suffer a decrement in their work. If they are told they did poorly, however, they will redouble their efforts and improve their performance. They do not want to fail, they just do not want to succeed. Men who suffer fears over achievement experience the following terrible conflict: Their desire to achieve constantly pushes them into achievement situations. Once there, they are driven forward by a desire to achieve and to avoid failure. But as they come closer to success, anxiety appears, and they must find a way to withdraw from the achievement.

The conflict between striving for and avoiding achievement often manifests in an inability to complete tasks. For example, the ultimate indication of success for students is graduation. One way the achievement-fearing student may deal with this evidence of success is by delaying graduation as long as possible. They put off making a decision about their major area until forced to by the college administration, then they often change their majors. They delay making a decision about what career they are planning for after graduation, or they frequently change their minds about their choice. These avoidances are a way to evade acknowledging that they will in fact graduate one day.

To avoid the success of graduation or even of doing well in an individual course, men who suffer achievement anxiety sabotage their performance. They may work hard and do well in the early stages of a course to ensure a passing grade, then they forget to do assignments or to attend exams, get ill before a class presentation they have prepared well for, or decide that a completed paper needs more work and thus do not hand it in on time, all of which result in a lower grade. If their intelligence allows them to do well despite their tardiness, their ultimate sabotage is dropping out of school. Alternatively, they may transfer to another school where not all of their previous credits are acceptable. Outright failure is thus avoided and they can continue to strive to achieve, perpetuating the cycle.

Carl, a twenty-two-year-old analysand, is an extreme example. He had already attended three different schools and was now in his fourth, a community college. As usual, Carl had started well and received good grades during the first year, but was on his way to failing most of the courses in the current semester, when he was referred to me for therapy by the school guidance counselor. Carl said that after completing the first year he had begun to skip classes and rarely studied. As we discussed the matter during our first interview, Carl seemed genuinely upset about his poor performance in school and worried about his future. When I questioned him about how he had dealt with his declining performance, however, it became clear that after he had calmed his anxiety by studying harder and improving his grades, Carl had quickly reverted to his old form and begun again to sabotage his performance. A common diversion for Carl was a part-time job at a department store, which he used to avoid schoolwork by working overtime whenever he was asked. He justified his behavior by rationalizing that his middle-class family could not adequately support him through college.

Perhaps Carl's most extreme avoidance of academic success occurred when he did not hand in a paper on time, the final requirement for a course in which he would have received an excellent grade. He asked for an extension and was given an extra two weeks. Carl missed that deadline too, again sought understanding, got another extension, and again failed to finish the paper. Each new chance presented what Carl saw as a greater demand for a better and better paper to make up for his previous tardiness. This only served to intensify his anxiety. The final weekend before his third chance, he could have worked hard, finished the paper, and still received his excellent grade. Instead he spent the entire weekend stocking shelves in the department store.

A significant failing in the adaptation of men who fear success, as exemplified by those who are unable to complete tasks, is indecision and the inhibition of competitiveness and aggression.

Decisiveness is a characteristic of the instrumental/active dimension and is traditionally associated with the masculine gender role. A man knows his own mind, makes quick decisions, and acts fearlessly. It is no wonder that when conflicts over achievement exist, paralysis in the individual's decision-making capacity also occurs.

We've all known men who are afraid to make decisions and try to get someone else to tell them what to do. The man will present all the data pertaining to a conflict and then ask for advice. To ease the other's anxiety we may give advice or ask a series of questions that helps clarify the issue so that a decision is obvious. The man, often with additional support and encouragement, makes the decision and acts. Unconsciously, however, he has never decided, but has identified with our cues as to what we think is the best decision. While the interaction has focused on helping the man make the best decision, what is frequently overlooked is the meaning being decisive has for the individual.

Often these men do not want to take responsibility for possible mistakes; if they can get others to give advice, they can then blame the others if the wrong decision is made. This is an avoidance of failure. A man conflicted over having traditional masculine characteristics, however, is not indecisive because of a fear of making the wrong decision. The rightness or wrongness of the decision is irrelevant; it is the meaning of making the decision itself that has significance. Symbolically, these individuals make an unconscious connection between decisiveness and masculine achievement, which arouses fear.

An Example: Joel

Joel, a twenty-three-year-old salesman, had experienced moderate success in his career. Yet he felt that his indecisiveness prevented him from fulfilling his potential in his professional and personal life. Joel could not choose a restaurant or movie without conflict; he would always ask the person he was with to choose. If Joel chose, he would immediately present himself with the alternative, which he would then experience as the better choice. The girlfriend he was with was, in his mind, always the wrong choice for the evening.

This conflict became excruciatingly obvious one day when Joel started for work in a rainstorm. First he decided to take the subway, as he was concerned that the streets would be slippery and he might have an accident. On the walk to the subway Joel thought that perhaps driving his car would really be the better choice. There was a garage in his office building, and if he parked there he would not get wet walking the three blocks from the subway entrance to his office. As he walked back toward his car he again worried about the danger of driving in the rain, decided that his original decision was really best, and headed back toward the subway. Within a minute he was walking back toward his car, having reversed himself again. Finally Joel realized that he was standing still in the middle of a downpour, unable to make up his mind in which direction to move.

Examining this incident in therapy led Joel to realize that either decision would have been appropriate. His concern was not that either decision would have been wrong. But making the decision and acting on it quickly would have made him feel confident in himself, like a strong man, and that possibility aroused Joel's anxiety that something bad would happen to him.

Joel belonged to a chess club, and his chess game gave valuable insight into his problems with achievement. Joel was often unable to defeat an opponent whom he believed he should have beaten with ease. He would miss easy moves at crucial points in games he was winning. Against superior players whom he could not beat, however, Joel played well.

On those occasions when even his errors did not make him lose, Joel noticed that he was more aware of guilt over damaging his opponent than pride in his victory. Often his guilty reaction, accompanied by imagined thoughts that onlookers were thinking critically about him, was so intense that Joel would refuse to play another game and withdraw from the tournament.

Joel had been taught to play chess when he was only five years old by his father, a fine amateur chess player. Joel's father had encouraged him to try his best and showed pride in Joel's developing skills. With a natural talent and love of the game, Joel, by the time he was ten years old, was already superior to his father and began study with a series of chess masters.

Joel's father was a very competitive man, and while he had encouraged Joel's early development as a chess player, he became angry and argumentative when Joel's abilities overshadowed his own. Joel, frightened by his father's outbursts and guilty for damaging his father's oversensitive pride, became afraid to play his best.

In therapy Joel became aware of his guilt for hurting his father, his sadness over his father's withdrawal of love, and the wounding of his own youthful pride by his father's stinging criticisms. Joel also became conscious of purposely sabotaging himself through poor chess moves against inferior opponents, who had unconsciously come to represent his father. When Joel began studying with grand masters of far superior ability, he felt relieved because they could easily beat him. He was then able to play his best without fear of damaging anyone or suffering their retaliatory aggression.

SELF-CASTRATION

As is obvious from Joel's example, the developmental origin of achievement inhibitions often resides in early rivalries between the son and his father. If the father is competitive with his son, the son's normal rivalrous feelings are heightened. Some fathers humiliate their sons when they compete. Others arouse guilt or threaten withdrawal.

In situations where severe intimidation exists, the equation between aggression and violence is reinforced. The child begins to withhold aggression out of fear of violent retaliation. The misconception that aggression must be violent is extended to assertion of all kinds. As an adult with ambitions intact but aggression inhibited, the son lacks the capacity to take effective action. He associates competition with the original rivalries of childhood. His attitude toward the father becomes transferred to other men. To recognize openly his interest in success carries with it the potential risk of retaliation by the parental competitor.

For men, the principal forms of unconscious fantasized retaliation are psychological castration and homosexual submission. Since in our society masculinity is associated with strength, dominance, and superiority, it is not surprising that people who suffer from conflicts over aggression and competition often associate success and decisiveness with phallic symbols of potency, which are then associated concretely with the penis. For such a man, being successful means having a large, adult penis. Having an adult penis, however, arouses his unconscious competition with his father. His defense against the resulting castration anxiety is self-castration. The individual experiences and presents himself as not having an adult penis. Sometimes this self-castration will manifest as a fantasy that his penis is too small to satisfy a woman; at other times he may be beset with homosexual fantasies. Such fantasies express the unconscious meaning that the individual should not be perceived as a man, but is really more like a woman. The self-castrating man understands "feminine" to mean passive and noncompetitive, and by expressing feminine fears he opposes the dangers inherent in striving to be masculine, which he sees as being competitive and assertive. These kinds of fantasies lead to anxiety symptoms, which often become accentuated after a successful experience.

An analysand who worked as a therapist manifested the above symptoms. He was afraid to progress in his own therapy or show his interest in professional subjects. The analysand fantasized that I would experience his ambitions to become an expert therapist as a competition for masculine supremacy and try to hurt him. This fantasy caused him to keep secret his intellectual, professional, and psychological growth. Instead, in treatment he manifested only his conflicts and weaknesses.

This man also fantasized that I was having affairs with my female patients. Ultimately he began an affair with the patient of another analyst. He suffered great anxiety telling me about this affair and fantasized that I was angry. His associations revealed his competitiveness with me. They indicated that he unconsciously considered his affair a victory over me and associated his success with having an adult penis. He wanted to become an expert in order to be a better analyst than I was. His fantasy was that then all my patients would come to him, especially the female patients. He further imagined that he and I would display our penises to the females and the women would consider his penis larger and more attractive. In the fantasy, I became enraged and threatened him with a meat cleaver. The analysand felt defenseless. Having an adult penis placed him in competition with me, the analyst/father, and brought up castration fear. He defended against this fear by presenting himself in a castrated manner, hiding his phallic potency.

Consistent interpretation of the analysand's fear of success in terms of his fear of competition with his father was followed by a dream: "I find my stolen shoes in a homosexual's shoe store. After I retrieved my shoes I was attacked by a bully with yellow hair who hit me on the buttocks with a tool."

He associated his shoes to his ability to maintain a phallic standpoint and the yellow hair to a lion and then to his father, who is a Leo. He experienced the dream as confirming his fear of having a masculine potency. During the following weeks he began to experience irrational anger toward men on the street, which subsequently turned into directed assertive feelings toward the abusive director of the mental health clinic where he worked. In time he became able to experience his own ambitions separate from his competitive feelings toward others and free of unreasonable anxiety.

Awareness of competitiveness and self-assertion not only arouses fear of retaliation but, since it may be symbolically equated with fantasied murder of one's parent, also arouses guilt. The consequent need to inhibit assertion can in turn lead to phobic behavior. If success is achieved, the need to undo the guilt, through suffering or paying penance, can result in a need for expiation, self-punishment, or masochistic adaptations. The unconscious need for punishment does not have to be connected to actual misdeeds; it may be connected to fantasies or wishes that are deemed immoral. We see this in people who inflict unnecessary injury on themselves, fail in their careers when they are about to succeed, or cannot let themselves enjoy anything.

One analysand's father died when the child was four. The analysand unconsciously fantasized that his sexual desires for his mother and aggressive wishes for the father had sickened and killed the father. As a consequence, the analysand felt he had won his mother but was guilty of patricide. He thus experienced terrible guilt whenever he successfully asserted himself. Feeling that he did not deserve to live for his heinous crime, he supposed that his life should be one of atonement through suffering.

THE MOTHER, ACHIEVEMENT, AND THE SON'S SHADOW

From the father, the typical dangers to the son's development of the instrumental/active dimension are aggression and guilt. From the mother, the danger comes from a different avenue—separation. Being left all alone is one of the greater threats in life. Even adults react with apprehension and tend to cling to a person they love when they know they are to be left. Young children, not surprisingly, react with fear to even brief separations; the threat of prolonged separation or abandonment can be traumatic.

In the presence of a responsive mother figure a young child is commonly content and, once mobile, is likely to explore his world with confidence and courage. Under such circumstances, a boy first learns to forage afield and return in triumph when he is crawling. Each of his small excursions becomes a lesson in accomplishment, not the fear of it. The boy is able to use his mother as a base camp for explorations in all directions, periodically returning to his mother for reassurance and recharging his emotional batteries.

By contrast, other mothers become anxious when their child tries to separate from them, and they cling to the child. Such mothers may rationalize their inhibiting behavior as a concern about whether their son will be able to "make it" in the world into which he is taking his first autonomous steps. They try so hard to keep their child from bumping his head that he never learns how a banged head feels, or how to overcome a setback. Further, the overprotective mother who swoops down regularly, with palpable alarm and fear, punishes the explorer emotionally for his adventures, and the child inevitably records the mother's sense of anxiety about his activity. The mother's attitude ultimately has an effect on the boy's feeling toward achievement in the physical world.

When my son was two to four years old, I belonged to a parent-child group that met once a week. The parents would sit around and swap stories about their children while the youngsters played. I recall one mother who was obviously quite comfortable with her son's tentative attempts to separate from her. She watched attentively and smiled as her son made small movements away from her into the unknown world outside her lap. By her attentiveness and encouraging smile she tried to ensure that her son's curiosity and explorations brought him gratification without serious harm. She seemed to understand instinctively that room to roam is particularly important to a small child, who is just forming an attitude toward relating to the outside world, and that to be successful a person must enjoy taking small, calculated risks and venturing occasionally into the unknown.

A second mother had difficulty letting her son separate. She had an anxious relationship with her son, an anxiety that became obvious when he tried to separate and function independently. When the boy tried to crawl away, rather than encouraging his attempt to relate to the outside world, she caught his attention and drew him back into the interaction with herself. She seemed to need her son to be in a clinging relationship to her in order to calm her own anxiety.

To separate from mother and confidently explore the environment a child must feel secure about its connection to the mother. When a child is uncertain about this connection, it tends to respond to new situations with fear. The mother afraid of her child's development may purposely or inadvertently threaten the child's attachment to herself by first holding on to the child and then defensively pushing the child into premature autonomy. Under such circumstances, the child clings to the mother rather than venturing forth.

This is what happened with the anxious mother in our playgroup. When her son would not return but continued his explorations, she became visibly upset. When he hurt himself, as children always do when they are first engaging the environment, she would turn a cold shoulder to him, as if to show him

that he could not get along without her. Her emotional un-
availability had the desired effect—the child's energy went into
wooing his mother rather than relating to his environment. As
a matter of fact, it appeared that his development itself caused
him anxiety. In contrast to the other children, who got involved
in their play, secure in their mothers' availability, this boy
would anxiously look back to see if his mother was still there.

Just as the responsive mother encourages the son's age-appropriate attempts to separate, the responsive father plays a vital role in helping the child separate from the mother and engage the environment. If the father is receptive and supportive
as the son moves away from the mother, the child will want to
identify with him as an alternative. The father's role is to draw
the son into the real world of things and people. He represents
the instrumental/active dimension—interest in and mastery of
the external environment.

Sometimes the father does not serve his function of drawing
the son into the world but is actively negative, frightening the
young child just at the stage when the boy is attempting to
separate from the mother. Rather than gently guiding and encouraging the youngster out of the comfort and security of the
relationship with the mother and into a relationship to the outside world, the fear generated by the father sends the boy back
into the relationship with her. The values represented by the
father remain undeveloped, not available, and even frightening
to the child.

As the next example indicates, the fear of separation from
the mother, due to the mother's implicit threats of abandonment and the father's criticism of the son's separation attempts,
can result in both an accumulation of the instrumental/active
characteristics in the shadow and a consequent fear of accomplishment in the external world.

An Example: John

John was twenty-two years old and addicted to marijuana when he first came to therapy. He had just graduated from college and was filled with anxiety over what to do with his life. He had studied writing in college, written an award-winning short story, and hoped to make a career related to publishing and writing. Two weeks before his first session he had got his first free-lance job copyediting a novel for a small publishing house. Despite extensive experience as an editor on the school newspaper in college, John completely botched the job, handing in a poorly cut, disjointed product to his superior. He was told that his work was amateurish, far below the level needed for his position, and that he should not expect any more work.

In discussing this experience during his first session, John recalled that when he woke up on the morning he was to begin his new job, he felt confident. He knew he was a good writer and an excellent editor, the two jobs he had to perform. Then, for no apparent reason, he was filled with panic. The fear was so great that he vomited. He felt alone, with no one to take care of him, in danger of annihilation. He recounted a dream he had that night: "I am taking a writing test. It is within my capacities and I am well prepared. But as the situation develops I get anxious and mess up by not paying attention. I could have paid attention if I wanted to."

While John had always thought of himself as a person afraid to enter the world because of fear of failure, he readily recognized that such a fear was not the issue in the dream; rather, the dream indicated that he could have succeeded by paying attention if he had wanted to.

John's earliest memories were of waking up in the middle of the night hearing his parents fighting. His mother and father had separated when he was two and a half years old. His mother told John that she had kicked his father out of the house because of her unhappiness over his work-related absences. She said that she was tired of taking care of her husband's needs and never getting her own needs satisfied.

John recalled how his father had criticized and humiliated him over his separation activities, making fun of his attempts to walk, yelling, and frightening John when he moved away from his mother. When John entered the "terrible twos," his father responded by yelling at John's negativism and aggression. Similarly, John's attempts to master the instrumental/active dimension were also met with derision. For instance, when John managed to accomplish a task, his father set the difficulty of the task higher so that it was no longer age-appropriate and then laughed when John was not able to master it. John's father helped to create a dangerous world outside mother, and John retreated back to the safety of mother's protection from the external world he had tried to enter. John's mother was a willing accomplice, comforting him, telling John how bad his father was, and reassuring John that he would be safe with her.

Over the next months John recalled early fears of being separated from his mother. He had been afraid to play with other children unless his mother remained in the same room and would cry hysterically if she tried to leave. He vividly recalled his panic over going to nursery school. He would do anything to cling on to mother.

John's life was suffused with the idea of restricting his development. Accomplishment and expansion created anxiety. He recalled severe panic attacks after graduating from high school and college. John now recognized that the compulsive smoking of marijuana began during one of his panic attacks after graduation from high school. Smoking marijuana was one of the few ways John could ease his anxiety. John's current fear of expansion was manifested in his living in a small, cramped apartment even though, thanks to a large trust fund, he could afford something larger; he also would not buy the computer he needed for his writing.

During the fourth month of therapy John recalled two dreams from the same night that helped to clarify the association he had developed between separation and achievement.

> I am at a reading where writers are reading their best short stories and poems. I read only the first draft of my short story, the draft that has all the material I had later cut and revised, rather than my finished story, which is very good.

> I'm in a gym with people I know. I'm working out on the equipment and doing it well. An older instructor asks me to do an exercise on the parallel bars that is far beyond my capabilities. I try anyway and fail. He laughs derisively and does the exercise effortlessly. I feel endangered and inhale some gas, which gives me the ability to float. I float to the top of the gym and curl up in the corner where the wall meets the ceiling. If I stay there the anxiety will go away.

In discussing the dreams, John related them back to his earlier dream the night before the botched edit and realized that he had sabotaged himself for fear that if he did well the ante would be raised until he could no longer perform adequately. Then he would be humiliated and criticized. John recognized this as the pattern that had existed with his father. He now understood that the expectation of humiliation had interfered with his willingness to expose his attempts at mastery, which would have indicated his desire to be competent in dealing with the external world.

The really curious thing was the ending of the last dream.

John associated the gas he inhaled with the marijuana he was always smoking, and the position he curled up in with a fetal position. When he was frightened as a child, John recalled, he used to find snug places—a corner in the closet, under the covers in his parent's bed, an old refrigerator box in the basement—and curl up in this position. He would imagine that he was being cradled in his mother's arms, and that image made him feel safe.

John's dreams provided the clue that marijuana served him as a substitute for the maternal process. John had begun to smoke marijuana habitually after he graduated from high school and suffered the first of the panic attacks, which he now understood to be related to accomplishment and separation. Subsequently, whenever John had to go into the world and take care of himself, especially when he was in danger of being successful, he smoked marijuana to calm his separation anxiety.

Smoking marijuana soothed John and temporarily relieved his anxiety. The momentary relief was like a soothing caress from mother, telling him that she would protect him from the dangerous world outside mother that his father helped create. Mother, too, had made the idea of entering the outside world frightening. By telling John of her reasons for kicking his father out, John's mother implicitly told John that if he were successful and ventured away from her or stayed away too long, as his father did on his business trips, she would not permit him back.

Often the desire to remain merged with the mother and not separate is unconscious and is replaced by a symbol of the mother that serves some of her functions. Whenever John felt himself satisfying his adult striving to develop, to go into the world and adapt, deal with his anxieties, and accomplish his goals, he would fear both his father's need to up the ante and his mother's threats of abandonment. He would retreat back to his mother by smoking marijuana, her symbolic equivalent. While high on marijuana he would be safe in mother's world, secure in a snug fetal position in a womblike enclosure. In his imagination he was then not separate from her.

THE SHADOW AND THE HAIRY WILD MAN

Fathers, through hostile competition and guilt, and mothers, through threats of abandonment, can cause the young boy to avoid developing and integrating such characteristics as assertion, competition, and instinctuality, all necessary to experience and satisfy the motivation to achieve in the external world. When such deficits in conscious development occur, the shadow appears in dreams of men in a primitive form. Robert Bly uses the image of the hairy wild man to express what is missing in these men who are frightened of their aggressive and sexual potency.[5]

The hairy wild man, according to Bly, represents forceful energy and resolve, assertive energy that Bly contrasts to machismo and cruelty. Wild-man energy is not focused primarily on domination and destruction, but is directed at a constructive engagement with the external world. In addition, wild-man energy, the phallic power with which men feel imbued when they have instinctuality at their disposal, is especially contrasted to the naive, passive, castrated men Bly refers to as "soft males." Soft men, influenced by the cultural upheaval of the women's movement, can read poetry and talk to their wives and girlfriends, but they lack energy, assertiveness, and the ability to make commitments. Bly does not believe that men should look to John Wayne or James Bond as role models. He spurns those caricatures of masculinity. Instead, he notes that almost every preindustrial culture projected in its myths and poetry an image of an ideal man as a forceful, spontaneous, primal being—a hairy wild man.

Much of the current men's movement involves efforts to bring to consciousness the qualities of the traditional masculine gender role that lay undeveloped and dissociated in the shadow. To that end, groups of men have been gathering in semiwilderness, apart from women, to engage in such activities as drumming and dancing around bonfires, hoping to free what is claimed to be a gruff, elemental "wild man" lying deep inside every ordinary male. Many such seekers of the "wild man" have not previously been able to develop in a healthy form the traditionally masculine side of the personality. They are either "soft" and femininized or macho—an exaggerated expression of the instrumental/active dimension. For them, the initiatory experience that occurs from going off into the woods and bonding with other men under the guidance of mentors is a necessary step in a developmental sequence. These men are at the important stage of development where the split between the genders must be emphasized and they must find a healthy, valuable masculinity with which they can conform. In itself, however, such discovery must be considered only a preliminary step in the development of masculinity, and certainly insufficient for becoming a male human being.

In discussing the hairy wild man, it is important to distinguish uncontrolled instincts, whether of aggression or sexuality, that are impulsively acted out from instincts that have been tamed, that is, disciplined by conscious meaning. The latter can be used to develop and express the characteristics of the instrumental/active dimension.

Some men who have never learned the importance of discipline from their fathers imagine that because they throw tantrums and use anger to dominate situations, especially with women, they are assertive and masculine. Similarly, they feel that acting out lust in an uncontained manner and without any concern for its effects on others is a further sign of their masculinity. After all, they and the masculine stereotype in our culture contend that men are always randy and ready to go.

In fact, the consciousness of such men is weak, as they do not have the ability to control their impulses consciously; they do not yet have the choice of going along with or holding back the reflexlike urges of arousal. The hairy wild man does not represent undisciplined, acted-out instinct. On the contrary, the image represents the instinct that can save the weak male whose image of masculinity has become identified with impulsive behavior.

The ancient Babylonian epic of Gilgamesh illustrates this point. When the myth opens, Gilgamesh, the ruler of Uruk, is behaving in a tyrannical manner. "Gilgamesh sounds the tocsin for his amusement, his arrogance has no bounds by day or night. . . . His lust leaves no virgin to her lover, neither the warrior's daughter, nor the wife of the noble."[6] The citizens of Uruk complain to the gods about Gilgamesh's arrogance and lust.

It is clear that Gilgamesh is behaving unreasonably. His aggression and lust are uncontained. He has sex whenever his lust demands and he lords it over others whenever his aggression urges. He is the picture of a man dominated by the desire aspect of instinctuality.

The goddess Aruru responds to the pleas of the citizenry, and Enkidu is created in the wilderness: "There was virtue in him of the god of war, of Ninurta himself. His body was rough, he had long hair like a woman's; it waved like the hair of Nisaba, the goddess of corn. His body was covered with matted hair like Samugan's, the god of cattle. He was innocent of mankind; he knew nothing of cultivated land."[7]

Here is an image of the archetypal hairy wild man: he is like the god of war, so he has lots of aggression, and he has never known cultivated land, which means he comes directly from the unconscious and has not passed through the ego identified with culture or conscious values. Most of all, Enkidu is defined by his long hair.

In primitive, animistic psychology hair is representative of the mana, the magic power of the personality. The location on the body where the hair occurs corresponds to the meaning attributed to this mana energy. For example, body hair is suggestive of the emanations of body power and animal instinctuality. Pan, the Greek nature and fertility deity, has hairy legs up to his loins. He is usually represented as a very sensual creature. Esau, the hairy son of Isaac, was a hunter and was depicted in legend as the advocate of the instinctual world and its pleasures. Long hair on the head can be representative of body strength. Samson and Absalom, who were both of gigantic strength, were Nazirites who were not allowed to cut their hair. The shaving of the hair, conversely, can mean loss of strength or renunciation of instinctuality. Samson lost his strength when Delilah betrayed the secret source of his power and his hair was shorn by his enemies. Similarly, to shave one's hair or cut it in a tonsure denotes the ascetic or the dedicated person renouncing the physical powers. This is one reason why priests of many religions shave their heads.

Enkidu's long hair and animal fur suggest that he represents instinctive potency and warlike aggressiveness. If we remember that Enkidu was created to be a companion and helpmate to Gilgamesh, we must wonder why Gilgamesh would need his help. He seems to have plenty of strength and aggression, as the citizens of Uruk are quick to complain about. But Gilgamesh does not have a disciplined aggression; he has no self-control. He does not create anything with his instinctuality; he is dominated by impulsivity.

Another important point is that Enkidu is created to aid Gilgamesh in his development. Here is the teleological element. In the normal developmental sequence, psychological reality is split into masculine and feminine, and males identify their masculinity with and develop the instrumental/active dimension. Self-discipline—the ability to relate to one's own impulses in an assertive manner—is a prerequisite for the development of the instrumental/active dimension and, ultimately, for security in the masculine gender role. Until the male can successfully accomplish this task of becoming a traditional man he cannot go on to the next task of developing into a male human being.

A man is meant to develop beyond the stage of impulsive acting out. If a man lacks self-discipline with his own impulses, the ability to be aggressive in a creative and constructive manner with the external environment is never allowed to develop. If a man is undeveloped in this way, however, the need for such development does not remain static; it exists as a dynamic potential in his psyche. The shadow is purposive; like all archetypes it has a directional component. The teleological purpose of the psyche, the development of wholeness, exerts its dynamic through the shadow. One of the ways this process is symbolized is through the image of the hairy wild man, striving toward union with the masculine ego-consciousness.

That is exactly what happens in the Gilgamesh story. First Enkidu has an initiatory experience while living with a group of shepherds in which his consciousness and discipline are developed; then he struggles with Gilgamesh, loses, and becomes his companion. After Enkidu's death, Gilgamesh discovers the terrors of mortality, tries to defend against that realization by seeking a herb of immortality, and when this fails becomes the hero he is meant to be, creating great cities and doing wonderful deeds.

Enkidu's initiatory experience during his period living with the shepherds is significant in terms of men's developing the kind of consciousness necessary to relate to their instincts in a disciplined manner. Initiation is a process in which people are helped to make transitions from one stage of development to another. To be initiated means to be transformed in some way. For example, in puberty initiations, young boys are put through a series of rituals by the older men in the tribe, which helps them to break the connection to childhood and mother and learn the cultural traditions and values of the adult males of the tribe. Common to many initiation rituals is the requirement to resist fatigue and go without sleep for long periods of time. These tests of discipline emphasize the awareness aspects of consciousness.

It is significant, then, that when he is with the shepherds, Enkidu functions as a watchman. While the others sleep, he must resist fatigue and stay awake. In his position as watchman, Enkidu captures lions and wolves that would otherwise eat the shepherds' livestock. The lion, as the zodiacal sign for the sun's greatest heat, is suggestive of frenzied desire. Wolves, too, are representative of the desire aspect of libido. For example, in German mythology the Fenris wolf breaks out of the bowels of the earth and swallows the sun. In ancient Rome, Lupa, or she-wolf, was the name given to harlots to indicate their predatory nature. Wolves and lions, then, in their negative aspects, represent frenzied desire that functions in an uncontained and even predatory manner.

The initiatory symbolism in the Gilgamesh epic—Enkidu's

staying awake and capturing lions and wolves—implies that an important part of masculine development is the ability to capture instinct. The image of capturing instinct, rather than killing it, implies that instinct is not to be repressed, but held on to by consciousness. To do so requires the development of self-discipline, the ability to experience an internal force coupled with choice in its expression. A man needs to experience instinctuality as a force that imbues his personality with vibrancy; at the same time he needs not to identify himself with the instinct. The conscious experience of aggression and sexuality is critical, yet the individual male needs to be differentiated from the stereotype of the angry man who destroys anyone who crosses him or the Don Juan who proves himself sexually at the expense of the humanness of others.

Yet it must also be understood that while a man needs to be initiated into traditional collective masculinity, that initiation can result in a loss of individuality. Once a boy is initiated into the rituals of the collective he becomes a man like the other men; he knows and believes what they know and believe, because that is what men know and believe and always have. While such initiation serves the positive purpose of helping men develop the full potential of their collective's traditional masculine image, it unfortunately places limits on them as human beings. To develop into a full male human being, further growth is necessary.

6 | Power and the Male Gender Role

The original division of psychological reality into opposites, including the polarity of masculine and feminine, occurs in early childhood; the split between the genders and the one-sided identification of the masculine gender role with the instrumental/active dimension reaches its zenith in early adolescence. Development then demands that a person experiences and integrates the human qualities represented by the expressive/passive dimension, previously shunned as representative of the opposite gender. But the transition to this next stage in the developmental sequence may be anything but smooth. Many men experience a great resistance. Men are remarkably fixed in their traditional gender roles and resist attempts to change their attitudes and behavior. Progress toward exploration and alteration of traditional gender roles originated with women and the feminist movement; men are only at the rudimentary stages of bringing consciousness to the one-sided masculine roles in which they have remained entrenched.

In trying to understand the resistance males have to changing their traditional gender roles, the interrelationship between the sociological and psychological is important. Inner experience, the psychological, is largely determined by the outer social environment. What people are permitted to experience is to some extent limited by what their society says is all right to experience. If, for instance, society's standards indicate that it is aberrant for a man to be submissive and normal for him to be powerful and dominant, the man will make an effort to behave in a powerful manner. If he is successful and achieves a position of power, he will feel positive about himself. If circumstances force him to behave submissively, he will feel inadequacy and shame. A man's attitude toward his own behavior and his feelings about himself are affected by the standards of his social environment. Only with great conscious effort can the average man free himself from cultural identification and develop an individual attitude toward his experience and himself.

An inner conflict, then, exists between the inherent drive to develop the personality and the values society holds for the masculine gender role, values that have been internalized as part of the persona. American society's standards for the masculine gender role are identical with those developed during the conformist stage, the stage in development when the split between masculine and feminine categories is greatest and the masculine gender role is identical with the instrumental/active dimension. While men are driven internally by the teleological urge to transform, they are at the same time constrained externally by social pressure to conform, and internally by the need to avoid feeling inadequate and humiliated, feelings that accompany the violation of internalized standards.

As we have seen, American society continues to associate power, influence, and dominance with the masculine gender role and weakness, helplessness, and submission with the feminine gender role. We can look at the identification of power with the masculine gender role and male resistance to change from two points of view. First, being powerful has positive aspects; power is more satisfying than powerlessness. Power allows the user to more readily satisfy needs, diminish insecurity, and increase self-esteem. Second, male entrenchment in exaggerated power roles functions as a defense against the fear of maternal power and feminine identification.

Power Is Satisfying

Power represents the possession of control, authority, or influence over others and events. It is a characteristic of the instrumental/active dimension, the set of activities designed to control and manipulate the external environment in order to achieve goals. Power is a normal part of everyday life, from the requests people make of each other to the demands that governments hand down to the citizenry. It is the ability to act physically, mentally, or spiritually to produce an effect. With power a person can exert control over circumstances, give direction, or resist the unwanted influence of others; with power an individual can make decisions and compel obedience; with power a person can obtain what he or she wants. To live life as one wishes requires that a person be able to have some power with which to influence situations.

The desire to accumulate power is a normal drive of the human personality. Alfred Adler, an early psychoanalytic explorer of the subject, suggested that it is only when this drive to have control over the events of life becomes excessive that problems emerge. The need for excessive power arises, he said, only when there is either an innate inferiority that needs to be compensated, such as a physical inferiority, or when a child has been reared so that he or she feels psychologically inferior. In these instances an inordinate need for control develops, a control not used for productive activity but defensively to compensate for painful feelings of inadequacy.[1]

My own experience differs from Adler's formulation. While

I find that excessive attempts to control can be compensatory to feelings of inferiority, I also find that people try to accumulate as much power as possible simply because of the benefits that accompany power. Not only does power provide some control over external events, but it is also significant in terms of a person's inner experience. Having or not having power affects the way people feel about themselves. For instance, a person who has power will feel competent; he or she can use that power to get things accomplished and satisfy needs. Because of their recognized ability to get things done, powerholders are likely to be frequently praised and flattered and to have their wishes carried out. Seeing their desires met and being flattered cannot but make holders of power feel good, especially in comparison with persons who are without power. As a consequence, the person who can wield power successfully will possess higher self-esteem than the person who is powerless.

Given the practical and psychological benefits that derive from the accumulation of power, it is not surprising that people seek it. What is unusual is that American society has identified this quest, at least in its overt form, almost exclusively with the masculine gender role. Power is expected of men, not women. Men are raised to believe that they have derived the right to influence others not from society but from biology— that is, that greater power is biologically inherent in their gender. This view of male rights has been supported by our language, laws, and institutions, which provide the male with the privilege of influence. Along with achievement in the external world, the accumulation of power is one of the defining characteristics of the masculine persona.

The perception of power as an intrinsic part of the masculine persona is readily confirmed by psychological research. On scales that measure characteristics commonly associated with the masculine and feminine gender roles, men are perceived as aggressive, not easily influenced, dominant, skilled and worldly, and acting as leaders. By contrast, the feminine gender role is associated with weakness and submission. The view of men as powerful develops at a very young age; by the time children reach the age of five to six years, they perceive men as having greater power, strength, and competence than women. This early perception of men as powerful remains central to men's definition of their gender role and does not diminish as they get older; a powerful image remains important to men, and failure to appear powerful can be a source of great anxiety.[2]

In fact, as well as in appearance, men do exercise greater power and influence than women. Men have greater power to reward and coerce, owing to their possession of most of the concrete resources in our society; they are looked to for expertise in most areas; they run our government, our military, our major corporations, and all our other institutions of significance. Men assume leadership and express their opinions more readily than do women, and people are more likely to follow the leadership of a male. In groups composed of males and females, research shows, men are more active than women, exert more influence, and assume roles related to leadership and power.[3]

Not only do men have more power than women, but they also exert power in different ways. Television programs, comic strips, and movies constantly depict men as exerting power directly; they use physical force and give commands. Women, on the other hand, are represented as indirect; they try to get their way by appearing helpless and dropping hints. Likewise, popular stereotypes portray men and women differently in terms of how they are influenced by the power of others. Men are expected to be independent and individualistic; women are shown to be gullible and yielding.

Whether people have power and whether they are direct or indirect in how they exert it are important in determining whether they get what they want and how they feel about themselves. People who exert power in a direct way, openly using the force at their disposal, increase their self-esteem. People who are indirect and manipulative conceal that they are the source of power. While they may be effective in the short run, users of indirect influence are not likely to view themselves as strong; their implicit recognition of weakness leads to a decrease in self-esteem.

Men's greater power and their direct expression of that power lead both sexes to evaluate males more favorably than females. For example, psychological research shows that both men and women assign a significantly larger number of favorable adjectives to males and a significantly larger number of unfavorable adjectives to females. In two studies, over 90 percent of male subjects and over 80 percent of female subjects said they considered men "superior" to women overall.[4]

The difference in self-esteem that results from such differential evaluation was observed by Adler when he wrote: "thus 'masculine' signifies worth-while, powerful, victorious, capable, whereas 'feminine' becomes identical with obedient, servile, subordinate. This type of thinking has become so deeply anchored in human thought processes that in our civilization everything laudable has a 'masculine' color whereas everything less valuable or actually derogatory is designated 'feminine.'"[5]

By now it should be clear why the original impetus to change traditional gender roles came from women. It was initially difficult for women to fight for change in their traditional role: they had to overcome resistance by men unwilling to give up power and status; they had to overcome feelings of deviance for failing to conform to sociocultural standards; they had to go against their own internalization of those feminine values, a process that aroused feelings of inadequacy and shame. The motivation for change was also compelling, however. Unconsciously, women were impelled by the teleological drive toward higher development. Consciously, it became clear to many women that identifying their gender role solely with expressive and passive values was limiting. They saw that masculine characteristics, such as power and its direct expression, were more socially desirable and resulted in higher self-esteem. In addition, they were becoming aware that economically the expressive/passive dimension left women without the wherewithal to satisfy their ambitions in the external world. Women came to see clearly the practical and psychological value associated with the characteristics represented by the traditional masculine gender role, and they wanted those characteristics for themselves.

Perhaps their recognition of the value attendant upon the traditional masculine gender role explains why women have always been freer to experiment with cross-gender attitudes and behavior than men. Boys show consistent and continuous development of interests appropriate to their gender through childhood and adolescence; girls go through an important phase during middle childhood when they show interest in the characteristics traditionally associated with the masculine gender role. Also, more females than males respond that they have wanted to be of the other sex at some time in their lives.[6] This indicates that cross-gender wishes derive not so much from faulty identification processes as from females' realistic perception of the relative social value and privilege of the other sex.

The qualities that females experiment with in their cross-gender activities are valued by society. Thus, while a woman may lose some of her traditional femininity by developing such traditional masculine characteristics as power, competitiveness, assertion, ambition, and a motivation toward achievement, she gains the rewards that accrue to those who efficiently use those qualities—financial rewards, power, and the increased self-esteem that comes with each.

It has been more difficult for men to change. The social opprobrium is worse for men who indicate an interest in the characteristics of the feminine gender role than for women who display such an interest in those of the masculine role. To be a "tomboy" is a positive quality for a young female; to be a "sissy" is a humiliating putdown for a boy. The characteristics traditional to the feminine gender role are devalued and do not bring increased social status; thus the man who displays them loses value in his own eyes and in the eyes of the collective. For a man curious about the experience of passivity, penetration, submission, or other aspects of the expressive/passive dimension, cross-gender experimentation would be defended against with the utmost intensity. Increased signs of power and control are the way to defend against such "deviant" curiosity.

By having and using power, men have based their self-esteem, at least in part, on power. Loss of power causes men to feel insecure in their masculinity, especially if they have failed adequately to fulfill other aspects of their gender role. Being powerless places them in the position of women, a position considered inferior. Since they do not have actual accomplishment from which to derive legitimate power, they fall back on the most superficial aspects of the masculine gender role, physical strength, to give them a sense of power and maintain self-esteem. Dominating women, devaluing women, accentuating differences with women, and believing they are better than women become ways to maintain their definition as men and their self-esteem.

An Example: Jerry

Jerry had been a drill sergeant in the Marine Corps for twenty years. After he retired from the service, he got a job with a company that provided security personnel to large corporations. Because of his experience commanding men in the service, Jerry was hired to train and supervise the work of some twenty men. He was married and had an eighteen-year-old son.

Jerry did not do well in his job. In the service he was used to giving orders and having them obeyed without question, and while this approach was somewhat effective during the training of the security officers, it was not effective afterward, when the employees became part of a union. With the power of the union behind them, the officers were not willing to acquiesce to arbitrary commands. For effective management, diplomacy and relational skills were now also required.

When a security officer refused to obey immediately or talked back, Jerry did not try to find out what the problem was, but would simply reissue his order in a louder voice. This did not work to gain compliance. The men began to make fun of him, calling him "Sarge" in a derogatory tone of voice. Jerry felt powerless and humiliated and threatened to beat up a couple of the men. The union complained to the management of the company, and Jerry was told that his job was in jeopardy because of his inability to handle his men effectively.

During this difficult period at work, Jerry began to drink heavily and became verbally abusive to his wife and son. He would mock them both, and when his wife began to cry he would mock her even more. Especially galling to Jerry was the sensitive nature of his son. Jerry made fun of the boy, calling him a sissy for playing the guitar and telling him he was nothing but a weak woman when the boy showed his upset feelings. The boy needed to go into the service, Jerry said; the marines would know how to make a man of him.

Around this time, Jerry was advised to get psychological help from the personnel director of the company where he worked and was referred to me by a colleague. After seeing Jerry in individual therapy for six months, I could tell that he was entrenched in a very rigid masculine gender role, a role that had been fortified by his long years in the military. His position as drill sergeant had accentuated power as an intrinsic part of his masculine role. The drill sergeants used to compete among themselves over who could be more arbitrary and controlling of the recruits they were training. When the sergeants would go out drinking they would brag to each other about their dominance and reinforce the idea that it was indicative of their masculinity.

Jerry's orientation toward power did not appear to be compensatory to unconscious feelings of inferiority. His history indicated no basis for assuming serious feelings of inadequacy: Jerry had been raised in a working-class environment by parents who, while not overly demonstrative in their love, were generally supportive and caring. Jerry had been an adequate student in high school, a good athlete, and popular, and he had had girlfriends. Rather than based on neurotic defense, Jerry's orientation toward power and control seemed a result of the working-class values with which he had originally identified, reinforced by the military subculture he had lived in for so long; both cultures had emphasized the intrinsic relationship between masculinity and power. Jerry's attacks on his wife and son appeared to be an effort to shore up his self-esteem, an attempt to show that he was still a man through the exercise of power over others. He had no history of being abusive to either his wife or son prior to his difficulties at his current job.

After getting to know Jerry, it seemed to me that, therapeutically, an alternative culture that emphasized different values would help Jerry to gain consciousness of the psychological relationship he had developed between power and masculinity. It was this connection that now was causing him to feel insecure; as a result of his loss of power at work he could not maintain his self-esteem by controlling others. I suggested to Jerry that he work in group therapy as well as attend his individual sessions. Jerry agreed. The group consisted of four men and four women.

Jerry's experience in group therapy was instructive. At first he dealt with group therapy as he would with small task-oriented groups in the service that had a practical problem to solve. Jerry would take charge, ask questions that elicited information, come to a practical solution, and then give advice in an authoritarian way. He expected the other members then to act to resolve the problem. Jerry mostly ignored what the females in the group had to say, especially when they tried to elicit feelings about the situation under discussion. While he ignored the females and their feelings, Jerry was openly contemptuous of the men when they showed their feelings. Especially obvious was his contempt for one man who was submissive to his wife.

The group members had been patient with Jerry, seeming to understand that his behavior toward them was not based on meanness, but that his insensitive comments and controlling behavior were due to beliefs that he still did not question. Their patience ran out one session when Jerry attacked the submissive man, who was crying over some hurtful incident with his wife. Jerry told him to stop acting like a woman and be a man. Jerry was shocked at the group's reaction to his comment—not only was he confronted by the women in the group for his insensitive and sexist remark but, even more surprising to him, the other men did not stand behind Jerry and agree with his position. They too said that Jerry's views of what men and women were like were primitive, especially his attitude about men having to be strong and powerful all the time. Jerry looked angry and confused when he left.

Jerry spent many weeks discussing this incident in his individual sessions. At first he wanted to leave the group; he thought that the men were weak and disturbed and that if the result of therapy was to turn men into women he wanted no part of it.

A dream he had helped to change his mind:

> I am big and strong, almost of giant size. Something is being built, houses or a city, and I am in charge. I tell lots of people what to do and they all obey me instantly. I feel proud. Then some natural disaster occurs, a hurricane or tidal wave. Things I had built or caused to have built are in danger of being wiped out. I try to build dikes to protect everything, but the water is rising too fast and will overwhelm all efforts. There is nothing I can do to prevent the disaster. I'm helpless and ashamed of my inability to control the situation. As soon as I realize this the scene changes. I am now normal size and working with a group of people to rebuild. It will be a lot of work, but we will get it done.

The dream showed Jerry the extremeness of his attitudes about masculinity and power. In the dream he felt like a giant when everyone obeyed him and the work got done. Loss of control, on the other hand, damaged his masculine feelings.

Jerry was ashamed in the dream when he was helpless to control the situation; his self-esteem as a man was on the line even in the face of a natural disaster. The dream helped Jerry begin to understand that there are things in life that he could not and should not be expected to control.

What was also significant to Jerry was that in the dream the process of rebuilding began only after his experience of shame and helplessness. Then Jerry was of normal size and working alongside a group of people, not commanding them. These images were very significant for Jerry; they began a process of conscious reflection that ultimately led to a change in his attitudes.

But first a sacrifice had to be made. In the dream Jerry did not know that his experience of shame and helplessness would lead ultimately to a rebuilding, and that a cooperative attitude could replace arbitrary power and also be effective in getting things done. Similarly, in his conscious life Jerry had to go through the process of giving up something that he knew to be of value, his lifelong derivation of masculine pride from power, for something that on the surface he considered less valuable, the acceptance of helplessness, a position he associated with females.

Jerry's conflict is not uncommon for men whose developmental process brings them to the point where they have to integrate the expressive/passive dimension, traditionally the province of females. Giving up the experience of unilateral power and the ability to exercise unilateral control is experienced as a loss; the exercise of power is something from which men have traditionally derived much masculine pride. While the experience of the expressive/passive dimension is ultimately broadening and deeply satisfying, initially it is often accompanied by feelings of inadequacy and shame. To feel helpless and passive are opposite to feeling powerful and active, and the recognition of those feelings causes many men to feel nonmasculine. In this sense, men have to sacrifice the immediate satisfaction they have traditionally derived from feeling powerful and accept the experience, albeit temporary, of shame in order to reach a goal that is intangible, at least at the moment of sacrifice. What they get in return for the sacrifice is the possibility of further psychological transformation—of becoming a male human being.

POWER AS A DEFENSE AGAINST FEMININE IDENTIFICATION

Another cause of resistance to change in the masculine gender role is the unconscious fear men have of the power of females and feminine identification. Men's age-old fear of female power is clearest in ancient myths and beliefs. Wolfgang Lederer, in his book *The Fear of Women*, has assembled a catalog of the fears and actions men take to defend against the power of women. The Norns and the Fates, female figures able to cut off the life of man, were prime examples. So was Pandora, the female gift whom Zeus sent to man as retribution for Prometheus's theft of fire from the gods; when she took the lid off her box she scattered all the evils through the world. Witches were irresistibly attractive and inhumanly destructive, as the inquisitors knew when they burned witches by the thousands across Europe between 1258 and 1782. Tribes around the world have myths of females whose vagina have teeth—and of heroes who learn how to master them. Menstrual bleeding is part of the mystery of birth, but almost every culture has incredibly detailed rules for avoiding what men once saw as a deadly curse, a curse of amazing variety. A menstruating woman kills one of two men she walks between, according to one passage in the

Talmud. Males respond to these ancient fears of female power by emphasizing their own power over women and by exaggerating the characteristics of the masculine gender role.

Some contemporary authors have suggested that male fear of females grows out of the long period of time during which children are raised by their mothers. As a result of spending so much time under her influence, children develop early identifications with the mother, whom they experience as powerful. In contrast to girls, who can continue to identify with their mothers, boys must suppress these initial identifications before a masculine identity can develop. In order to separate from the maternal identification and diminish the mother's power, these authors reason, men devalue and exert compensatory power over females. Separation is enhanced by emphasizing differences and devaluing what men are not like. But it is not only the real and fantasy-distorted powers of women as objects that must be struggled with; any qualities and impulses within men perceived as feminine must also be suppressed. Consequently, in order to overcome the fear of female control and maternal identification, men defensively demean women and feminine characteristics and identify with and assert the very power they fear in women.[7]

The idea that adult males identify masculinity with power in order to defend against an underlying fear of female power and maternal identification has merit, especially when looked at from the vantage point of the unconscious. From this point of view, boys would actually be expected to be more similar to the mother than to the father. That is only natural, since the earliest identifications are with the mother. As the child separates from the early merged relationship with the mother, the child must find a way of replacing the mother's provision of love and nurturance when she is absent. The child achieves this through identification—by internalizing the mother as an image, the child can have its mother ever-present and perfect.

The consolidation of core gender identity, the affective and cognitive revelation that one is a male, occurs at the same time that the boy is struggling to disengage from the mother, on whom he still depends and with whose person and qualities he longs to identify and emulate. The young boy strives to be like his mother at the same time that he comes to cherish his new-found masculine identity.

At this moment of conflict, when the boy recognizes that he is male and not female and seeks masculine models with whom to identify, the father's role is vital. He helps the child differentiate from the mother by representing the world that the child is entering. If the father is receptive and supportive as the boy moves away from the mother, the child will want to identify with him as an alternative.

Even when an appropriate paternal identification occurs, however, the earlier identifications with the mother continue to exist. The boy does not become more like his father than like his mother. For boys, what is more similar to their fathers are the characteristics of the masculine gender role that they emphasize, not the total personality. Characteristics that are like the mother continue to exist, either as part of the male's conscious personality, recognized as derived from the mother, or in the unconscious.

Traditional feminine characteristics that are integrated into the conscious personality do not necessarily lead to a defensive or rigid masculine gender role, especially if the attitude toward the feminine in general is positive. Masculinity and femininity are not inherently adversarial, especially after early adolescence. Traditional feminine characteristics that remain unconscious because of defense, on the other hand, can lead to psychological conflicts. Negative attitudes toward the feminine often cause the early maternal identifications to remain unconscious after a boy has developed the traditional masculine gender role. Defense mechanisms are employed to prevent the feelings of masculine inadequacy and anxiety that would be aroused by consciousness of the maternal identifications. These defense mechanisms prevent the subsequent transformation of the masculine gender role.

Two situations commonly lead to inner conflict and the development of defenses against the early maternal identifications and subsequently, as a result of generalization, to other characteristics of the personality considered feminine. First, a situation that combines a traditional masculine identification with a devaluation of the female and feminine characteristics can lead a boy to deny any similarities to his mother. Second, an absent or devalued father may lead to an insecure masculine gender role and fears of female domination and feminine identification. A compensation of machismo—an exaggeration of the traditional masculine attributes—often results as a defense.

IDENTIFYING WITH THE FATHER AND DEVALUING THE MOTHER

In circumstances where a boy is raised in an environment where the traditional masculine characteristics are emphasized and valued, the boy identifies with those attributes and develops the traditional masculine gender role. The flexibility of that role to change is dependent on whether a defensive or developmental identification was its basis—that is, whether the role was internalized as a result of fear of the father or as a loving emulation. In addition, the ability of the masculine gender role to evolve, especially in relationship to the traditionally feminine characteristics, is dependent on the value placed on women and feminine attributes.

In situations where women and the feminine gender role are devalued and the masculine role adopted is traditional, especially if the masculine role is identified with as a result of fear of the father, defensive denial is common. Typically, the man will deny that he is anything like his mother. If characteristics of his personality are pointed out that are similar to his mother, the man will deny that she is the source of those aspects and will insist that the traits are really an identification with his father.

One patient and his sister, two years younger, were raised almost exclusively by their mother, an immigrant from Poland. The mother was a passive, submissive woman, very traditional in her ways, but also quite depressed and negative toward herself and women in general. She would say that women were weak and worthless and could do little but clean a home and serve men. My patient and his sister were frightened and revolted by their mother's self-hate, but also felt guilty and protective toward her.

The father, also a Polish immigrant, worked long hours seven days a week. When he was not working the father liked to play cards with his friends. Occasionally the father came home when the children were awake; during those instances the father postured in a primitive masculine mode, dominating the children, especially his son, and demeaning his wife. "You stupid cow" was an expression my patient often recalled his father using toward his wife. My patient feared his father, felt the need to protect himself from his stinging comments, but also was fascinated and envious of his powerful position in the family.

This man started therapy because of serious problems with

gambling, depression, and his marriage. In therapy he demonstrated a brittle masculine gender role based on a defensive identification with his father. When not depressed, he imagined himself a powerful person, as he imagined his father, respected and even feared by family and friends as a result of his ambitions and achievements in life. In fact, his achievements were quite limited. The patient often bragged about his gambling and workaholic ways, despite their obvious destructive effect on his life, saying he picked up those habits from his father; he was also proud of his emotional inexpressiveness, recognizing that similarity, too, with his father.

What this man did not recognize was a more fundamental identification with his mother. He had her depressive, self-hating character. Moreover, the woman he had married was the one who was really similar to the patient's father; she was dominant and cruel to the man and to their children. Even though the patient did not like his wife's treatment, especially her abusive comments to their children, he passively submitted to her domination over the family.

When I would attempt to bring some consciousness to his identifications by pointing out his similarities with his mother, the man would get outraged and deny my observations. He would then defend further by overemphasizing the characteristics of his personality that he considered similar to his father. One day he dreamed: "My father and I are on a balcony together, and my father is giving a speech to people in a square below. I feel pleased being associated to such a powerful person. My father's hair was combed like the hair of Joseph Stalin." Rather than being horrified by an image in which he associated himself with a tyrant like Stalin, my patient was quite proud. He used that image for months to defend himself against my observation that he was identified with his mother's passivity and was dominated by his wife, the one who was really like Joseph Stalin.

AN ABSENT FATHER AND AN INTRUSIVE MOTHER

A defensive attitude toward the early maternal identifications, and toward females and femininity in general, often develops in males when the father is absent physically or psychologically, especially if the mother is dominant or devaluing of her husband. A brittle masculine gender role based on power over women may develop; such a role is unconsciously designed to compensate for an underlying fear of female domination and feminine identification.

In the child's development of a gender role, the father functions as the primary representative of the outer world, defining what sort of role is acceptable. The father's failure to mediate this role has a different significance for the boy and the girl. If a young girl remains identified with her mother, she suffers a loss of individuality in her feminine development. She has a female identity, but it is a replication of her mother's. A boy, on the other hand, has to switch his primary identification from that of a female to that of a male, otherwise he loses his gender identity.

The importance of the father in helping a boy separate from his earliest identification with the mother and give him a male identity is seen in the puberty initiation rituals of the so-called primitive societies. Common to these male initiation rituals are the separation of the young adolescent from his mother, who ritually mourns the son as if he were dead, and the son's isolation among the males, often for months or years, where he undergoes a period of instruction characterized by various ordeals. During this period the boy is taught his adult masculine role. When he returns to the tribe the boy, now considered a man, usually lives in the men's house. These initiation rituals emphasize the importance for boys of breaking the connection with mother in learning to be men.

When a mother is intrusive and controlling and the father, owing to absence, indifference, passivity, or weakness, does not fulfill his initiatory function of helping his son separate from the early identification with the mother, the son's masculine development is disturbed. Not only does the boy fail to develop a secure masculine gender role, but his inner image of the feminine becomes inadequately differentiated from the image of his mother. The male does not grow up free to experience women as something other than the dominating femininity of the mother.

A common problem that develops, as a result of such circumstances, is an unconscious fear of being female, overcompensated by a defensive masculine role, as if by taking the masculine role to extremes the boy could overwhelm the feminine control and identification he so fears. Proving that they are not effeminate is a major preoccupation of such paternally deprived men. They compulsively reject anything that they perceive as related to femininity. Their fear of a feminine identity contributes to their need to control anything female outside themselves and anything feminine inside. Such defensively masculine men frequently engage in a Don Juan pattern of behavior, defining and exhibiting their masculinity by their relationships with women—for instance, by how many different women they can have sex with.

Common to these men is a fantasy that the psychoanalyst Ethel Person calls the fantasy of the "omni-available woman."[8] This fantasy is characterized by a woman who is always available sexually, forever lubricated, forever ready, forever desiring.

The fantasy suggests an overabundance of women whose primary interest and sole function is sexual, ensuring that the man will never be humiliated. They are completely under the man's control, always available and never rejecting. The women are automatically satisfied and require no special stimulus. Since these women are easy to please and experience great pleasure, they assuage a man's self-doubt.

AN EXAMPLE: ROBERT

Robert came to therapy because of a need to dominate women. In addition to compulsive masturbatory fantasies of the "omni-available woman," Robert was involved in sadomasochistic sex. Any self-assertion by a woman threatened his masculine self-image, and he responded with rage and control. His primary intent, however, was not to hurt the woman, but for her to recognize his power and masculinity.

Robert's father had left the family to fight in World War II shortly after Robert was born. His mother and father had decided to marry and have a child after the father realized he was to be inducted. The child was to "remind" the wife of her husband while he was gone. The mother had hoped for a quiet daughter to keep her company during the lonely years of her husband's absence. She insisted on calling her son Roberta.

Robert's father returned home safely from the war when Robert was four years old. He was a passive man, easily dominated by his wife, and he spent as little time at home as possible. The marriage did not work; by the time Robert was eight years old the parents divorced. Robert's mother found solace for her feelings of abandonment and loneliness through her son. The mother continually discouraged signs of separation and masculine development in Robert, not allowing him to play ball or running games with the neighborhood boys. Instead she would insist that he play quiet games of exploration in the house or help her with the cooking.

During the fifth grade Robert missed so much school due to "sickness" that the school administration insisted that Robert and his mother meet with the school psychologist. It became clear that Robert's absences from school began when he developed some minor ailment, and his mother treated the condition as being of much more consequence than it really was. Robert was kept at home, ostensibly to convalesce, but was gradually presented with a picture of himself as being unfit for the rough world of school and as being, therefore, in constant need of his mother's care. Unkind teachers, bullying boys, and chronic ill health were inculpated as the villains of the piece.

When Robert reached adolescence he rebelled against his mother's attempts at domination. Rather than be the shy, emotional, introverted person she encouraged, he overcompensated and forced himself to be extroverted and athletic. To be masculine became an obsession with Robert. He broke bones and acquired scars in sports at which he was never proficient. As an adult he impaired his health on daring exploratory trips into the jungles of Brazil; he took up parachuting and learned to skydive. He made a career of conquering and abandoning women. Any sign of emotion he squelched for fear of being taken over by his mother's demands on his personality and losing his precarious masculine identity. In defense against his fear of being dominated by his mother, he became a caricature of a man.

The initial phases of Robert's therapy were characterized by his parading his sexual conquests for my admiration. These episodes were especially extreme when he felt insecure in the face of a woman's assertion or if he had experienced "feminine" feelings of affection or intimacy. In his fantasy, I admired and valued his dominating behavior, respected his macho masculinity, and was somewhat envious of his conquests and control over women.

During this initial period, I had various countertransference reactions to Robert. I felt the desire to educate him about proper male-female relationships, to instruct him on the proper way to treat women. Once I actually acted this out and suggested he treat a particular woman more as an equal. My remark was met with a tirade about weak men castrated by women. At other times, I identified with his projected father and felt unmasculine and once even wondered if I should have an affair to prove my masculinity.

During Robert's second year of therapy, while he was sitting in the waiting room, a female analyst from an adjacent office replaced a picture on the waiting room wall with a new one. Robert stormed into his session muttering about "dominating bitches who feel they have the right to control everybody." "Everybody," in this instance, turned out to be me, the passive, weak wimp. "Why do you let the bitch from the next office control you?" he demanded. "What right did she have to replace your picture with hers, and not even ask permission? Her personality is taking over and you are too weak to even care. I bet you're dominated by your wife at home."

After this tirade, I suggested that the waiting room was like his young personality, which had been intruded on and dominated by his mother, and he was angry because he felt that I was like his father, incapable of asserting myself and rescuing his masculinity from his mother. The session ended in silence.

In the next session Robert brought in three dreams that helped him realize what he feared and struggled against: female domination and feminine identification.

First dream: "There is a dog on a tight leash led by a lady. I feel that the dog is myself. I'm furious at being tied to my mother. I can't tell whether the dog is male or female."

Second dream: "I'm going to a Caribbean island for a vacation. A fat butch dyke-type woman in authority won't let me on the airplane even though I'm in the front of the line and there are seats. I'm full of rage but feel weak and helpless to do anything about it. I'm wearing a dress."

Third dream: "Inside a fence is a monster animal. It is me. Some women outside the fence are making me fight with another beast. It was for their amusement. I kept running around saying: 'Do I have to? Please don't make me do it!' I'd run back and fight and then run back and say: 'Please, no more.' Then one of the women said: 'Here's your reward. You can play with your little tin can.' So I played with it like a little puppy and then they made me go back and fight again. She was making me do it to entertain them."

In analyzing these dreams it became clear to Robert that his fantasy of the "omni-available woman" as well as his sadomasochistic sexual domination were attempts to repair his damaged masculinity and cover his fear of women and feminine identification. While he acted out wishful fantasies about power, control, potency, and willing females, his fears were typical of the man afraid of female power: impotence, lack of skill, female rejection, and homosexual dread. He attempted to assuage his masculine self-doubt through the collective male fantasy of macho sexuality, in which control over the feared woman is sought through sexual mastery.

I pointed out to Robert that what was missing in the dreams was a strong masculine presence. The dreams consisted solely of Robert and powerful women. There was no male figure to nurture, protect, and guide him.

My observation helped him begin to realize that rather than demeaning his father, Robert really wanted to idealize him. Similarly, rather than putting me down, Robert wanted me to be the strong man who would initiate him into manhood and rescue him from his fear of being the girl his mother always wanted.

The insight that what he really wanted was a closer relationship with me aroused a new level of anxiety. The desire for intimacy and affection with another man implied that he was homosexual, and that his mother had actually succeeded in turning him into a woman. In addition, he imagined that I was repulsed by his need for intimacy and would humiliate him. During this period of the analysis, Robert experienced the depths of the masculine insecurity that underlay his dominating masculine role.

One night Robert dreamed: "I am playing ball with a man. The game is competitive but not aggressive. He is better at the game than I. I hope the other man will be my friend. I want his company and help. Perhaps he'll teach me."

After this dream, new fantasies began to emerge in which he and I are doing active things together. Robert began to imagine us doing carpentry or playing golf, activities at which, in his imagination, I was proficient and aided his development.

When Robert's feelings of intimacy toward me first began to emerge, my countertransference matched his feared expectation. I was upset with myself over my hostile feelings and my thoughts of how weak and needy he was. It was only after I could disidentify with his projection of the macho masculine image, and connect to my own feelings of being a nurturing man, that I could accept and lovingly relate to his tentative reaching for a masculine mentor.

CONCLUSIONS

As with the other men discussed in this chapter, Robert's early efforts to develop a masculine gender role were shaped not only by societal attitudes but by the unequal power relationship between his parents. Robert's mother dominated his passive father. The Polish immigrant parents of another man had an opposite relationship. Either way, the relationship between a man's parents has a large effect on his attitude toward women and his ability to recognize within his personal psychology characteristics considered feminine.

By contrast, when the boy has both an involved and respected mother and an involved and respected father, he is then exposed to a wider degree of valued and adaptive characteristics. He feels pride in his basic gender role orientation and comfortable enough in himself to be relatively flexible in his responses. Research indicates that a positive father-mother relationship results not only in a healthy masculine gender role but also in boys who are able to be flexible in experimenting with traditional feminine characteristics. Boys capable of such exploration had fathers who not only were masculine but also participated in the traditionally feminine role of child care, displayed to their sons the traditionally feminine qualities of emotion and expressiveness, and supported and valued their wives and the mother-child relationship.[9]

Nancy Chodorow, a psychoanalyst with an interest in social psychology, suggests that one way to change men's responses to women is to have men participate as deeply as women in raising children.[10] If we were to do this, Chodorow reasons, boys and girls would identify equally with both parents and would then have to separate from figures of both genders. Men might then be less obsessive about their masculinity and less compulsive about devaluing women. The unconscious fear of women that is really fear of maternal power would diminish. Men would no longer have to defend themselves by defining women as secondary and powerless.

The problem with this argument is that it does not account for the boy's developmental need to identify with his father and be unlike his mother as part of the normal course of his gender development. In separating from the mother it is natural to devalue what one wants to be different from. Chodorow is quite right to argue that an absent father leads to a brittle masculinity that compensates through domination of the feminine. But I disagree with her further contention that having a father to identify with leads to a better attitude toward the feminine, because then both father and mother are rebelled against and disliked equally. Having a father to identify with, especially a respected father, allows the son the opportunity to fill out his masculine identity and feel secure in his gender role. Is from this position of traditional identity that he has the security to accept those aspects of his nature that he had previously shunned as feminine.

What is really necessary, I believe, to liberate men from their fear of female power and feminine identification is for the father and society in general to value the qualities traditionally associated with the feminine. As the boy separates from his mother and develops his masculine gender role, it is critical that he also adopt a positive attitude toward the mother and the feminine characteristics he has incorporated from her, even as he is denying that they are part of himself. When the boy is secure in his masculine gender role, he can return with a positive attitude of rediscovery to something of value from which he was temporarily alienated.

7 | Submission & Masculine Transformation
Redeeming the Anima

An abundant literature explores the theme of power, control, and aggression. Their relationship to masculinity, femininity, the motivation to achieve, self-esteem, and other areas of behavior and psychological life is well documented. The paucity of research on the theme of submission stands in marked contrast. Outside of its association with femininity and lower self-esteem, the topic of submission has consisted mostly of clinical studies on sexual perversion, and those studies have focused almost exclusively on female masochism. Does this paucity indicate that submission is a less-prevalent motivational factor for human beings, especially for men, than the motivation to exert power and control? Or is it an indication of the devalued position that submission holds for our society?

To submit means to yield oneself to the authority or will of another, to put oneself in a subordinate or secondary position. While such behavior is evident and somewhat acceptable in females in our culture, going under the name of feminine passivity or, in its unacceptable form, female masochism, it is definitely antithetical to the masculine gender role. In our culture, men consider submissive behavior inferior and reject it as an aspect of their own psychology; it arouses humiliation if experienced. The masculine gender role is characterized by power, dominance, control of oneself, and, even more masculine, control of others.

Alfred Adler suggested that the drive to exert power and control over the environment exists in all human beings. If a drive for power exists, might not a drive to submit, its opposite, also exist as a coequal? After all, a normal aspect of cognitive functioning is to divide psychological reality into oppositional categories and, further, Jung said that consciousness develops as a result of the integration of the opposites. What happens to the process of integrating opposites when social values identify the masculine gender with one of the opposites, power, and the feminine gender with the other, submission, and movement between opposites, a process critical for transformation, is restricted?

The absence of an overt need to submit in the conscious daily life of ordinary adult males does not mean that such a need is lacking. Rather, this human need is unconscious in males, unfolding its effects in disguised forms: men project the urge to submit onto females and consider it a feminine characteristic.

To understand submission we can examine the meaning it has been given in different cultures, its relationship to transformation, and the fate submission has met with in our own culture. In addition, two important pathological manifestations can result from suppressing the drive to submit. How these symptoms actually symbolize the underlying need for submission and transformation makes up the latter part of this chapter.

INITIATION AND TRANSFORMATION

Since submission is considered a feminine characteristic, the need to submit is commonly represented by a male's assumption of the position of a female: dressing as a woman, pretending to have a female sexual organ or body part, or taking the receptive position in male homosexuality are all symbolic of male submission. The same acts and images are also commonly associated with male initiation rituals and the idea of transformation.

Initiation, whether into a new age group, secret society, or spiritual vocation, involves procedures for helping and guiding one through important transitions in development. To be initiated means that one is to be transformed in some way. Initiation always involves a symbolic process of death and rebirth. In archaic thought, death, the return to the original unity of existence, expresses the idea of an end, or the final completion of something. From this original state to which the initiate is returned, life is engendered. The initiatory death is considered a clean slate on which new life can be written.

In male puberty initiations, the old way that has to die is the connection to the mother and childhood. The new way that the initiate is to be born into is the way of manhood. The young initiates are taken from their mothers by the men who teach the boys the cultural traditions and values of the tribe. The young boys learn how to behave as adult men and are only then considered to be human beings. When the initiates return, they remain separated from their mothers and live from then on with the men.

In these male rituals of initiation, in which young boys are taught the ways of the masculine, the symbolism of the feminine often has a place of central significance. The Masai and Nimba tribes of Africa, for instance, practice the ritual of dressing the novice in women's clothing during the initiation ceremonies that transform the young boys into men. Similarly, in the Babylonian myth of Gilgamesh, Enkidu is dressed in the clothes of a female harlot who leads him like a child to a shepherd's encampment, where he is transformed from a wild animal into a man.

Being given a female organ or body part carries a similar significance of putting a male into a female position. For example, during the initiatory ordeal of subincision the urethra is slit the length of the penis. By this means, the novice is given a female sex organ. The Boubia tribe of Australia refer to the novice who has had this operation performed as "one with a vulva."

Mircea Eliade suggests that one purpose of the initiatory ordeal of subincision is obtaining fresh blood. The symbolic meaning seems to be that as a woman cleanses herself of her old blood through her menstrual flow, so the novice, by bleeding from the "new vulva," will be cleansed of his mother's blood and thus experience the death of his childhood connection with mother. Then the initiate's blood will be regenerated with man's blood. Thus, through the process of a menstrual expelling the novice experiences a death of the connection with mother and a transformation into a new man.[1]

In modern dreams we often see this sort of initiatory symbolism when a man is about to undergo a significant change or resists an inner need to transform. For example, an analysand who was resisting the anxiety inherent in separating from his mother dreamed: "I enter my childhood home in San Diego. It is overflowing with shit because the toilet is not working properly. I'm going to have to clean it up. In the middle of the room surrounded by shit I see an erect penis that has been slit on its head where the opening is."

Six months later, as the same analysand was beginning to experience his own positive masculine energy, he dreamed: "I see an image of myself as a woman. I know that it's me even though I'm also outside it looking at it. She is wearing a dress but also has a beard and male features to her face."

Homosexual and pederastic relationships are another symbolic way, common to initiation rituals, of putting men into the female position.

During festivals celebrating the initiation of puberty, Kiwai Papuans practice anal coitus on the young to make them tall and strong. It is believed that the mana of the older male is transferred to the initiate by such rituals.[2]

Similarly, in the ancient Dorian world, pederasty was a central factor in the upbringing of boys and youths; it was a means of transmitting *arete*, the best qualities of the Dorian nobleman. The phallus symbolized *arete*, and through the pederastic act the grown man's valuable qualities were transferred to the boy. The aim of the pederastic ritual was to make of the boy a man with strength, a sense of duty, courage, and all the other noble virtues.[3]

In the Dorian world, the homosexuality of the pederastic relationship had nothing to do with effeminacy. On the contrary, among the Dorians the aim of initiation was manliness in its most pronounced forms. The age difference between the lovers was always considerable: one was a grown man, the other still an immature youth. The youth worthy of love was eminent in respect to manliness and decency. The older man, valued for his manliness, passed his *arete* to the youth through his semen. Men cultivated pederasty and active heterosexuality at the same time. Men who stuck exclusively to boys and who did not marry were punished and ridiculed by the Spartan authorities and treated disrespectfully by the young men.

The Dorian and Kiwai Papuan rites were real and had genuine effects on the character, qualities, and capabilities of the novice. The ability to change and develop in the direction of being like the older male was furthered not only by an admiring, respectful, and loving relationship with that person but also by the symbol expressing the qualities of the model. For the young Dorian and Kiwai Papuan, the phallus of his tutor was a comprehensive image of all the latter's qualities that he wanted to acquire. Being placed in the position of physically receiving the valued qualities through the semen of the tutor aided the initiate in his efforts to change in the desired direction.

The preceding images of being symbolically turned into a woman during male puberty initiations all connote the idea of bisexuality. Eliade says that the theme of bisexuality represents an attempt to recover the primordial situation of totality and perfection in order to then proceed forward.[4]

The idea being unconsciously expressed in these puberty rituals is that a male has a better chance of attaining a particular mode of being if he first becomes, symbolically, a totality of male and female. From this perspective, dressing in women's clothes, having a female sex organ, or taking the receptive position in homosexual intercourse puts the individual into a hermaphroditic state. All imply a loss of differentiated masculine identity. By dressing in women's clothes, the male does not become a female, nor does he cease to be a male by assuming the receptive position in homosexual intercourse; rather, he becomes, symbolically, a totality of male and female, an undifferentiated unity. From this undifferentiated condition the boy continues his development. In the puberty rituals, for instance, the boy learns the values of his collective and develops into a traditional man.

Puberty initiation rituals emphasize the differences between men and women and are an essential part of men's learning to be masculine in a collectively acceptable way. Differentiation into oppositional categories and identification with one of the categories are necessary processes in masculine development. They result in only an intermediary stage of development, however. Further initiation is subsequently necessary if men are to heal the split between masculine and feminine and develop into male human beings. The identification with collective ideas of masculinity has to die and the man has to recover the qualities split off and left undeveloped as "feminine" so that he can be born into full humanness.

Humiliation

From this brief survey it can be seen that voluntary submission—the acceptance, symbolically, of the position of a woman—is related to the process of initiation. It is experienced as a necessary and valuable aspect of a ritual whose goal is transformation. The value of the person who undergoes the initiatory process is increased; through learning the values of the masculine collective the boy is transformed into the man.

Not all acts of submission are voluntary, however, nor do they have the symbolic meaning of transformation. In some circumstances, submission is experienced as a humiliation.

Power is often expressed between men by one man's forcing another into a submissive position and treating him as if he were a woman. In such circumstances, the person forced into the submissive position knows that the purpose of his submission is not positive but a humiliating surrender to domination. Being forced to submit does not increase the value of the person so forced. In contrast to the ancient Dorian ritual, where the more powerful man transmitted his *arete* to the younger male, the man who dominates another man imparts humiliation with his semen; the male forced to submit is dirtied, and it is by his devaluation that the man who dominates attains honor and value.

The domination of one male by another may be an archetypal pattern, an idea that was elaborated more fully in chapter 2. Male domination of other males can be seen most commonly in other species, especially in hierarchically structured animal groups such as baboons and chimpanzees. Among these primates weaker males present their rumps to dominant males as a signal of submission. When a male baboon feels threatened by a stronger male he wards off the danger by assuming the attitude of a female in heat. He exposes his hind parts to the superior male, who then mounts the submissive one, imitating the act of mating.[5]

Similarly, in ancient Scandinavia it was not considered shameful to force another man into the position of being used sexually as a woman. It was only shameful to be the one forced. Of primary importance to the ancient Norsemen was the power balance between men. What was decisive was the implication of being inferior in power. Such an inferior man was *argr*, the crudest term of abuse in Old Norse. This term indicated not only that a man was effeminate but also that he submitted himself to being used sexually as a woman.[6]

In contemporary Western culture, except in unusual circumstances, such as prison conditions, heterosexual men do not rape other men. Power and domination over women is often acted out through rape, however, and while not acted out physically between heterosexual men, the ancient meaning of *argr* still echoes in the modern-day man's fear of being "screwed." The concrete act of being taken advantage of carries the symbolic meaning of being forced into submission by another man. To be "screwed" by another man is an expression of weakness, a cause of disgrace to a man who feels he should be any man's equal. To take advantage of another man, on the other hand, is a sign of superiority in strength and rank and is symbolic of mounting an inferior male. For that reason, many homosexual men refuse to be on the receiving end of sodomy; they consider it feminine and thus inferior. They want to be in the position of the more masculine penetrator.

An inner conflict exists between an unconscious need to experience submission and a deadly fear of it. The experience of voluntary submission is a necessary aspect of the process of transformation; because of current cultural stereotypes that identify the need for power with masculinity, however, all forms of submission by men are resisted and considered feminine or homosexual. When submission occurs, it is experienced as forced and humiliating.

A clinical example will illustrate the conflict between the need to submit and the fear that accompanies it. The example shows how a repressed need to experience submission appeared in an analysand as a symptom of a terrifying fear of helplessness and an obsessive curiosity about being dominated. At the same time, the analysand's symptoms could be understood symbolically; they pointed to his underlying need for submission and transformation.

An Example: Bill

Bill came to therapy after he became obsessed by the idea that a minor argument he had with his wife would go on forever. He imagined that his wife would become more and more irrational and that the only way to prevent the continued deterioration and subsequent breakup of the marriage was for him to submit to her position and admit that she was right. She would then be the dominant person in their relationship and terrible things would happen to him. To calm his anxiety, Bill had to find some way to place limitations on the situation with his wife.

After Bill finished describing his fear of his wife's irrationality and domination, I asked him if there were other examples in his life of this fear. Bill said that loss of control was a common source of anxiety for him. Any time he was not in control of a situation he felt a danger that events would deteriorate and that he would be helpless to prevent a major calamity. For instance, Bill said that he owned and managed a two-family house. Both tenants paid their rent late. Bill feared that one of the tenants would never pay and that he would be helpless to control the situation.

I asked Bill why he was panicked and obsessed with only one of the tenants, since he had said that both paid their rent late. Bill said that while he felt annoyed with the upstairs tenant about her late payments, he attributed the lateness to circumstances beyond the tenant's control; he felt assured that the rent would arrive before the month's end, as it always had in the past. That knowledge of the situation limited his anxiety.

The downstairs tenant, on the other hand, was a man who Bill imagined paid his rent late purposefully in order to frustrate him; it was the tenant's way of dominating and humiliating him. Bill said that unless he could force the tenant to abide by the rules, the tenant would never pay the rent and there would be nothing Bill could do to stop him. The man's aggression would go out of control, forcing Bill into an ever more humiliating and helpless position. These imaginings made Bill angry and made him want to dominate the tenant in return.

I pointed out to Bill that, from what he said, loss of control meant helplessness; another person would have power that would be used to subjugate him. Helplessness resulted in submission and submission meant weakness, inadequacy, abuse, and humiliation. Helplessness never meant being taken care of by a stronger force.

Over the next months, Bill described a painful adolescence spent in a tough working-class environment where masculinity was defined by physical violence and domination. While physically large, Bill had been a sensitive boy who defended against his sensitivity by adopting the macho attitudes of his milieu. He became a bully who joined in the domination of the weaker kids. In describing this period of his life, Bill related proud tales of gang wars and feigned courage in the face of violence as well as guilty feelings for having tormented weaker boys. Finally Bill talked about a humiliating experience that he had never before discussed with anyone.

While jogging on the indoor track of his high school gym, Bill had pushed a smaller boy out of the way and begun to bully him. Another student had intervened and told Bill to stop. Bill had tried to intimidate the second student, who then invited Bill to fight it out after school. Bill had met the other student, now accompanied by a group of his friends, in one of the school's bathrooms. Soon after the fight started Bill had been seized by an unaccountable panic and tried to end the fight. The other boy had refused to allow the fight to end. Bill had felt increasingly terrified, completely unable to fight, and pleaded with the other boy to leave him alone.

The other boy had said, "Get on your knees and beg."

To the accompaniment of the derisive laughter of the other boy and his friends, Bill, compelled by his now uncontained panic, had done as he was bidden. His shame had been complete; he had been *argr.*

After a moment's thought, Bill said: "No, my shame was not really complete. All of these years I've wondered what I would have done if he had taken out his cock and demanded that I suck on it as the final humiliation. I don't know why I haven't been able to get that thought out of my mind. I had submitted so much by then, allowed myself to be so humiliated and dominated, I don't know whether I'd have had the strength to resist." Then after another moment's hesitation, Bill added: "Or would have wanted to."

The night after that last session, Bill dreamed: "A group of women live in a patriarchal culture, like in the Middle East. One is chosen by a man to be his wife. The man then worries whether he made the right decision. The woman who is chosen is calm."

In our discussion of his dream, Bill said that the men were dominant over the women, as was natural in Middle Eastern culture. Only the men in the dream had to deal with choice, being right or wrong. The woman who is chosen as a wife is calm because she knows her life is in the hands of fate; she submitted to a power stronger than herself.

One issue the dream raised pertinent to his conflict over helplessness and submission, I suggested to Bill, was that his fear of being dominated, for instance, by his wife, might mask a desire to be under someone else's control. The woman in the dream was in the position of a slave. She could relax into passivity, have decisions made with no possibility of error, be chosen rather than having to choose. Since an intense fear can sometimes be indicative of an unconscious wish for the thing that is feared, I wondered if the woman might not represent a part of Bill that wanted to experience passivity and if the fear of submission might not mask a wish to submit.

Bill intellectually understood the idea that submission could give someone pleasure and relief from tension; at least he understood how women could have such pleasure. He was a man, however, and men did not experience such a desire. Men were dominant, like the Middle Eastern men in the dream. Submission was the antithesis of masculinity. Bill experienced submission only when it was forced on him. It was something that he fought against, and if actually forced to submit, he felt great humiliation.

"Perhaps that is the only way you can make submission acceptable, having it forced on you against your will, as you did in the high school bathroom," I suggested.

Next session Bill reported the following dream: "I'm with a friend who is bisexual. He goes into a building while I wait outside and comes out later with clothes torn and very beat up. He had gone in there for the very purpose of getting beat up."

With great shame, Bill admitted to a lifelong curiosity about the experience of those forced to submit. He discussed a story he had read as a young adolescent about an aboriginal woman in Australia kept on a leash to be used by the local ranch men whenever they wanted relief. Bill recalled a movie he had seen around the same time, *The Pawnbroker*, in which the main character's wife had been made a sexual slave by the Nazis, to be used by the soldiers who were taking a respite from battle. More recently, Bill had been fascinated by a scene in the novel *Lonesome Dove* where a young female was captured by brutal Indians who beat her and used her sexually. Bill also wondered about homosexuals who went to clubs where they were tied up and sexually abused.

I commented that in Bill's examples the person forced to submit was in the sexually receptive position commonly associated with women.

"It isn't the brutality that's fascinating," Bill responded. "When I was younger I experienced that sort of control over pets, and to a lesser extent women, and I do not really feel drawn to it anymore. Plain physical domination that leads to death or people just being beaten does not really intrigue me. There's still some curiosity about dominating others, using them sexually without feeling and then leaving, but not much. It's too much like masturbation, and I feel guilty to others and myself if I take advantage of individuals."

"For some reason," Bill went on, "being completely under someone's sexual control, used by them whenever they want, fascinates me. Since you'd be completely without control over events, completely helpless, there is no point in resistance. All you could do is submit and let things happen to you. Do you dissociate under those circumstances, remove yourself from the body? Does the person controlled enjoy the experience once they let go? Is there pleasure in that experience somewhere? I've often wondered if this curiosity isn't behind the idea that men have that women would enjoy being raped if they'd just relax and stop fighting. I bet it's a projection of their own desire to feel dominated."

As Bill became more aware of his urge to submit he became obsessed by dominance-submissive fantasies. He masturbated frequently to pornographic images of mistresses and slaves, with himself in the position of the submissive person. After a while, masturbation did not satisfy the compulsion, and Bill began to visit prostitutes with whom he could act the slave. The prostitutes would order Bill around, tell him that he was bad and deserved to be punished, beat him, and make him beg for mercy. Occasionally Bill would have intercourse with these women after the dominance-submissive ritual was finished, but usually he left without having intercourse.

At first it seemed as if Bill's submissive behavior was a ritualized punishment for mistakes. His visits to the prostitutes for punishment were always preceded by a serious depression over some error that he had made. On top of the punishment inflicted by the female in the dominant position, Bill suffered additional punishment from the bad feelings he felt for having engaged in the "perversion."

In Bill's image of masculinity men were strong physically, emotionally, and financially. Being physically and emotionally strong meant dominance: a man dominated others either by physical strength or by the strength of his personality. A man was not needy but self-sufficient. Bill, by contrast, was inadequate simply because he needed to come to therapy; therapy indicated both that he was not self-sufficient and that I was a stronger personality. What Bill had was financial strength, having made a large amount of money in real estate. That is why making an error, which meant losing money, was so damaging to his masculinity. Any decrease in his assets, no matter how small, was a decrease in his store of masculine feelings of sufficiency.

Our understanding of his compulsion to act out submissive behavior to dominant women as a punishment for errors that he considered nonmasculine made sense to Bill and brought conscious agreement. It ultimately proved superficial, however, and led to little change in Bill's compulsive behavior.

When the conscious mind resists the deeper compensatory meaning that the unconscious is trying to impart, a fantasy will be often repetitive, because the resistance is preventing the fantasy from being finished. The individual will be aware of one level of meaning, but will not realize that allowing the fantasy to continue would permit another level to emerge. Such proved to be the case for Bill and his dominance-submission fantasies.

Bill liked to visit pornographic theaters and watch sadomasochistic movies. A special favorite was one where a group of men captured a woman, tied her up, and raped her repeatedly.

This scenario was the opposite of Bill's fantasy of submitting to a dominant woman and was reminiscent of his earlier fantasies of women as slaves. It provided a clue to the deeper compensatory meaning of Bill's dominance-submissive rituals.

I asked Bill who he identified with in the movie.

"I'm the leader of the men," he responded.

"Was the woman afraid?" I asked.

"At first," Bill replied, "until I had sex with her."

With great embarrassment Bill said that after the movie, when he fantasized about it, he imagined that the woman who was raped was so satisfied sexually by him that she changed from being afraid and resistant to a willing sexual slave—she would do anything so long as Bill continued to have sex with her.

This caused us to go back to the previous fantasies with the dominant woman. What happened after Bill was beaten by the woman? Bill had never taken the fantasy any further. I urged him to let his unconscious complete the fantasy. Bill was silent, as if watching an inner movie, and then responded that the prostitute became aroused by beating him and wanted him sexually. Bill was so sexually proficient with her and she was so completely satisfied that she changed from a master into a willing sexual slave.

Inherent in these fantasies was sexual adoration not only from the completely satisfied women but from male observers. In the fantasies, other men were always about. In the pornographic gang rape fantasy, the other men had also forced themselves on the tied-up captive, but she resisted and was traumatized, experiencing it as a rape. When it was Bill's turn, the woman was transformed, clearly filled with sexual pleasure, which the other men observed. The men were filled with admiration and envy for Bill's prowess.

In another fantasy, a dominant woman chooses Bill to be her slave out of a group of submissive men, all of whom are far more attractive and well built than Bill. She chooses him because she can instinctively sense his sexual potency. After she dominates Bill, they then copulate in front of the group of male onlookers. The dominant woman is so satisfied sexually that she is transformed and becomes Bill's slave. The other men recognize and are in awe of Bill's sexual ability.

Since these fantasies of sexual adoration occurred after Bill had made an error, errors he considered proof of his lack of masculinity, it was clear that Bill compensated for his feelings of masculine inadequacy with fantasies of great phallic potency. As the compensatory meaning of these fantasies emerged, Bill's compulsive need to act them out disappeared. He realized that he really did not want to be beaten, he wanted his masculinity to be adored and worshiped.

There was one element in the fantasies, however, that was not explained by the insight that Bill's unconscious dominance compensated for his feelings of masculine inadequacy. Not only did the females in Bill's fantasies become his sexual slaves because of his phallic potency, but they were also transformed from a primitive condition to a more developed state.

For example, in one fantasy Bill is a drug addict in a drug den where women give themselves to men sexually in return for drugs. The women are mechanical and unfeeling, letting themselves be sexually used in order to support their drug habits. After sex with Bill, however, a black prostitute is so sexually fulfilled that, for the first time in her adult life, she discovers feelings and is transformed. She no longer wants drugs, learns to respect her body, and develops her feeling and emotional life.

According to Jung, each individual has an individuation

path, a direction in which they are meant to develop if they are to fulfill their potential as a unique human being. This teleological element of the psyche is expressed through symbols; inherent in each symbol is the anticipation of the individual's future development. Normally we think of symbols as images that appear in dreams, myths, and fairy tales. But neurotic symptoms are also symbols; they give us information about what is wrong with the personality and provide clues for the developments necessary to cure the condition that gave rise to the symptom.

Sexual imagery in dreams can often be understood by the symbol of *coniunctio*—union with another figure. This image often carries the meaning that the dreamer needs to integrate the qualities associated with the figure with whom he or she is united in the dream; the dreamer must develop and make a part of his or her conscious life the qualities represented by the image. Similarly, when a sexual symptom exists, the person that one unites with physically is often representative of an aspect of the individual's unconscious.

As his analysis proceeded, Bill began to realize that the prostitutes he submitted to in reality and the primitive women in his fantasies both really represented aspects of his own psychology. Just as the primitive women in the fantasies were transformed by the union with Bill, so Bill had to develop the qualities in his personality that he considered feminine and that had been left in an undeveloped condition. Bill's fascination with submission represented a symbolic need to transform the inner feminine image, the anima, by developing and integrating the characteristics symbolized by her image. That developmental process proved to be a source of significant change and much suffering for Bill. But before I describe some of Bill's experience of change, the archetype of the anima needs to be discussed.

ANIMA

Jung adopted the idea of bisexuality, that people are composed of the qualities characteristic of both sexes. Biologically, "it is simply the greater number of masculine genes that tips the scales in favor of masculinity. The smaller number of feminine genes seems to form a feminine character, which usually remains unconscious because of its subordinate position."[7] The psychological manifestation of biological bisexuality are the contrasexual archetypes: the anima for men and the animus for women. Like all archetypes, the anima and animus represent the tendency to create an image in response to certain human situations.

The anima concept is complex. At various times Jung used the term to refer to the soul, to the personification of the unconscious, to the projection-making factor, to the feminine principle, to the fourth function, and so on. It would take us too far afield to discuss all of those issues; here I will limit myself to the general relationship between the anima and masculinity.

Jung is contradictory about the source of the anima's characteristics. In some instances, Jung attributes inherent characteristics to the anima and equates the anima with an archetypal feminine principle, Eros. Because the qualities and capacities associated with Eros are unconscious, they are inferior (undeveloped), and consequently, men are not naturally equipped to be related. The consciousness of men, on the other hand, is equated with an opposing archetypal principle, Logos, which, Jung suggests, specially equips men to discriminate, clarify, reflect, be objectively detached, and obtain self-knowledge. For women, the situation is reversed and the opposite norms apply to conscious and unconscious. To quote Jung: "I use Eros and Logos merely as conceptual aids to describe the fact that woman's consciousness is characterized more by the connective quality of Eros than by the discrimination and cognition associated with Logos. In men, Eros, the function of relationship, is usually less developed than Logos."[8]

At other times Jung describes the anima as the tendency to form an image of what is female, the image being defined by the culture. He says: "We must therefore think of these images as lacking in solid content, hence as unconscious. They only acquire solidity, influence, and eventual consciousness in the encounter with empirical facts, which touch the unconscious aptitude and quicken it to life. They are in a sense the deposits of all our ancestral experiences, but they are not the experiences themselves. . . . An inherited collective image of woman exists in a man's unconscious, with the help of which he apprehends the nature of woman."[9]

In this instance Jung is clear about differentiating the characteristics of the anima from cultural norms. He indicates that, for men, the anima represents the possibility of experiencing women in a human way. The anima does not contain specific characteristics, however; the inherent nature of the feminine is not the way it is imagined in any particular culture. Rather, the specificity of the anima comes from the encounter with the facts of women. It is the predisposition to experience women that is inherited; what is experienced depends on when, with whom, and where the experience occurs.

THE RELATIONSHIP BETWEEN THE PERSONA AND THE ANIMA

The persona and the anima complement each other. Those qualities that a man is capable of having as part of his conscious personality, but that are unconscious because of their association with the opposite gender, become associated with the contrasexual archetype. Jung:

> As to the character of the anima, my experience confirms the rule that it is, by and large, complementary to the character of the persona. The anima usually contains all those common human qualities which the conscious attitude lacks. . . . If the persona is intellectual, the anima will quite certainly be sentimental. The complementary character of the anima also affects the sexual character. . . . This contrast is due to the fact that a man is not in all things wholly masculine, but also has certain feminine traits. The more masculine his outer attitude is, the more his feminine traits are obliterated: instead, they appear in his unconscious.[10]

The anima contains those qualities that are rejected or not integrated into the persona owing to gender considerations. During the process of gender development, qualities not considered masculine become associated with the feminine and remain as undeveloped potential in the unconscious. Thus the same culture that determines the gender aspect of the persona also, by means of the dynamics of the unconscious, determines the nature of the anima. A man is defined by what he is, his masculine role, as well as by what he is not, the qualities and characteristics rejected and left undeveloped because they have been defined as feminine.

In an earlier chapter on the persona, I showed that one of the more significant factors in the development of the masculine gender role is the father. The son consciously imitates and unconsciously identifies with his father; the son's masculine persona is partly a function of these two processes. The father also affects the development of his son's anima. Just as the son identifies with and develops in himself what is masculine in the father, he avoids developing what is not developed in the father. Thus what the father considers nonmasculine, by and large, is viewed the same way by the son. These nonmasculine qualities, left undeveloped, become associated with the anima in the son. Insofar as the son is a replication of his father and does not have an individual masculinity, his anima will replicate the anima of his father. In addition, the mother provides the son with an example of what is feminine, that which the boy is not to be like if he is to develop as a man. The son's anima is thus also patterned on the mother's femininity.

ANIMA AS THE UNDEVELOPED

In general, men develop those characteristics that society says are appropriate to their gender role and either do not develop or actively repress those characteristics that society says belong to the feminine gender role. These qualities and characteristics are not inherently masculine or feminine, but they are culturally labeled as such.

The idea of the anima as representative of that which is inferior or undeveloped appears in three ways in Jung's writings.

1. Aspects of an individual's personality may be chronologically undeveloped. As the personality develops, fragments are left behind in a childish state, suffused with powerful infantile affects. These infantile aspects of the personality can lose their motivating effect only by being reunited with the adult consciousness. The anima, as psychopomp, points the way toward the childhood regression and ultimate transformation. Jung says that "the steps and ladders theme points to the process of psychic transformation, with all its ups and downs. . . . The

journey with father and mother up and down many ladders represents the making conscious of infantile contents that have not yet been integrated."[11]

For example, since emotions and feelings are considered feminine in our society, most men have not made a conscious effort to differentiate and learn to express them. As a consequence, many men have undeveloped emotional lives and react to situations emotionally as they did when they were children. Since undifferentiated emotional reactions are considered feminine, it is natural that the anima becomes the carrier, in a childlike form, of qualities such as neediness, instinct, and emotionality.

2. The contrasexual archetypes serve as psychological functions that relate the ego to the unconscious. According to Jung, many of the contents of the unconscious that can be integrated into consciousness are personified by means of the contrasexual archetypes. By personifying contents through images that can be perceived by consciousness, the anima and animus serve as a bridge between conscious and unconscious. But the anima and animus can serve as psychological functions only if the disparity between the positions of conscious and unconscious is not too great. If a great disparity exists, the contents personified by the anima and animus are summarily rejected by the ego, which refuses to accept that such contents exist in the total personality. The bridging function of the contrasexual archetypes then breaks down and the anima and animus become personified and behave like split-off personalities. Jung:

> [The] anima and animus is essentially a psychological function that has usurped, or rather retained, a "personality" only because this function is itself autonomous and undeveloped. But already we can see how it is possible to break

up the personifications, since by making them conscious we convert them into bridges to the unconscious. It is because we are not using them purposefully as functions that they remain personified complexes. So long as they are in this state they must be accepted as relatively independent personalities. They cannot be integrated into consciousness while their contents remain unknown.[12]

3. The anima is related to typology and the inferior function. According to Jung, consciousness is characterized by two attitude types, extroversion and introversion, and four functions: thinking, feeling, sensation, and intuition. Generally, each person has one dominant attitude type and two dominant functions through which they relate to the environment. The other attitude and functions are inferior, that is, unconscious and undeveloped. Jung:

> The anima also stands for the "inferior" function. . . . In the psychology of the functions there are two conscious and therefore masculine functions, the differentiated function and its auxiliary, which are represented in dreams by, say, father and son, whereas the unconscious functions appear as mother and daughter. Since the conflict between the two auxiliary functions is not nearly as great as that between the differentiated and the inferior function, it is possible for the third function—that is, the unconscious auxiliary one—to be raised to consciousness and thus made masculine. It will, however, bring with it traces of its contamination with the inferior function, thus acting as a kind of link with the darkness of the unconscious. . . . The fourth function is contaminated with the unconscious and, on being made conscious, drags the whole of the unconscious with it. We must then come to terms with the unconscious and try to bring about a synthesis of opposites.[13]

While typology is supposed to be gender neutral, the thinking and sensation functions have in fact become associated with the masculine gender, while feeling and intuition are now considered feminine. As a result of these cultural biases, men more often than women make a special effort to develop their thinking, or to at least make it appear as if what they are saying is a result of thinking. In addition, men try to relate themselves to the sciences, to fill themselves with facts and imagine themselves connected to "objective" reality. Feeling and intuition, on the other hand, have become associated with the feminine and left largely undeveloped in men. As a consequence, the anima is generally characterized by undeveloped feeling and intuition and, since the psyche personifies unconscious contents by means of images, the inferior functions for men appear as women.

THE DEVELOPMENT OF WHOLENESS

The cognitive differentiation of people into male and female and the subsequent development of a gender role is a necessary stage in development. For a young male, what is most important to develop is the persona, to learn to be masculine in the traditional way so that he can make his way in society. It is not normally possible for a person to learn to be both masculine and feminine at the same time. Jung said, "To present an unequivocal face to the world is a matter of practical importance: the average man—the only kind society knows anything about—must keep his nose to one thing in order to achieve anything worthwhile, two would be too much."[14] During the process of developing a masculine gender role, the characteristics considered feminine are avoided and left undeveloped. This is not harmful to the young. Jung observed, "Younger people, who have not yet reached the middle of life (around the age of 35), can bear even the total loss of the anima without injury. The important thing at this stage is for a man to be a man."[15]

It is only later in life that the absence of the qualities associated with the anima become significant for a man's life. That is when the teleological drive for wholeness inherent in the psyche assumes importance in a man's life.

One aspect of the development of wholeness involves the integration of contents that have become dissociated from consciousness. The person is confronted with affective tendencies, impulses, and fantasies that he or she had not been willing to recognize previously. The general rule is that the more negative and resistant the conscious attitude has been to the unconscious, the more repulsive, aggressive, and frightening is the face that the unconscious contents assume.

This general rule helps to account for one of the reasons that men resist the teleological urge to integrate the anima. The identification with the traditional social concepts of masculine and feminine is an important part of normal gender development, as is the devaluation, for men, of the feminine gender role. When men develop their gender role to the accompaniment of excessive disparagement of the opposite gender, however, these same social values interfere with the revaluation of the feminine gender role, which is a necessary prerequisite for the man's further transformation. The more a man has devalued the feminine as negative and weak, the more the contents of his anima will appear as repulsive and frightening when the teleological drive causes her contents to be presented to the man's ego consciousness for development and integration. The coming together of the opposites of masculine and feminine is experienced as a violation of all reasonable considerations, and the man is appalled. Anguish and suffering is experienced in the form of fear and feelings of inadequacy and shame.

Men who have a fixed image of masculinity lack temporality—the idea of change over time—in their viewpoint, and that lack forms the core of another resistance to integrating the anima. Men with a fixed traditional gender role can change comfortably only within the constraints of collective standards; they can only develop or add to the traditional masculine characteristics incorporated during the stage of conformity. When the teleological urge demands a more radical shift, a fundamental alteration of the personality that results from the integration of the traditionally feminine attributes, they often experience a fear of dying.

Symbolically, the image of death is a normal accompaniment to radical internal change. For something to transform, what currently exists has to disorganize and then be reorganized in a new form, affected by the contents integrated. The disorganization is symbolized by images of death, and the reconstitution by symbols of rebirth. The experience of death is normally accompanied by depression. A person who confuses the symbolic experience of death with physical death will resist the depression that necessarily accompanies the dying aspect of the process of transformation.

For instance, Bill held the view that an essential aspect of his masculinity was that he be powerful and dominant. His symptoms then forced him to face a new psychological fact, an urge to submit, which he eventually understood to indicate the need to redeem the anima, that is, to raise an inner female image from a primitive to a more developed condition. Concretely, to Bill this meant that he needed to discern and develop in himself the attributes that he normally considered feminine and make them a part of his own conscious psychology. Over the course of his therapy, as he made successful efforts to be affected by this insight, a fundamental modification took place in Bill's gender role and in his total personality. Not only did his view of his gender role change, but he also began to view himself as a male who was larger than his gender role. Bill ceased even to consider the attributes that he was developing in himself as feminine; they became aspects of human beings. He began to experience himself as a human being who was male.

This process of change was accompanied by much suffering, characterized by depression and the fear of death. During this phase of the analysis, when Bill's masculine persona and his identification with its values was being strongly affected by the integration of the anima, Bill suffered from painful hypochondriacal and paranoid symptoms. He experienced the death aspect of the process of transformation not symbolically at first but concretely; he believed that he was dying from a terminal disease. Sometimes Bill feared cancer; at other times his heart would palpitate wildly and he would swear he was having a heart attack. Bill also imagined that his wife was trying to poison him or harm him in some other way. Only when his dreams showed Bill that the death he was undergoing from integrating the anima was symbolic (the poison he imagined his wife would kill him with was actually the contents of the anima he was developing and integrating) was he able to recognize that he feared not literal death but the death that comes from psychological transformation.

HOMOEROTIC ANXIETY AND THE TRANSFORMATION OF THE ANIMA

Over the years I have encountered in my clinical work a significant number of men who suffer from what I call "homoerotic anxiety." They are not homosexual. Homosexuals are considered to be men who have a predominant romantic and sexual relationship with other men, either through activity or fantasy. Even when they live a heterosexual life, they are aware that their primary attraction is to other men. By contrast, men who experience homoerotic anxiety enjoy sexual relationships with women, have never, or rarely, had sex with men, and yet experience anxiety about the possibility of being homosexual.

The view generally held by psychoanalysts is that homosexuality is a pathological condition. That attitude is derived from the theoretical conception that a homosexual orientation is engendered by faulty parenting; the son fails to separate adequately from the mother and consequently fears closeness to women, or inadequately resolves the Oedipal conflict and does not properly identify with the father. The homosexual object choice is one attempted solution to the conflicts engendered during these developmental stages.

The traditional Jungian position on male homosexuality is similar to the psychoanalytic position in its emphasis on the struggle to separate male identity from the effects of the mother. The Jungian theoretical position is as follows: The normal archetypal relationship in the family is reversed, in that there is a strong predominating influence of the feminine. If that influence leads to a pathological dependency on the feminine, there develops an identification of the ego with the anima. Longing for masculine guidance, the young male overcompensates by associating only with men, as if to reinforce the masculine principle in the face of the original overweighting of the feminine. Essentially, then, homosexuality is an attempt to overcome, by means of compensation, a matriarchal psychology where the Great Mother is unconsciously in the ascendant.

Support for the traditional psychoanalytic and Jungian viewpoints can be found in amplifications that show how exclusively male societies originate in matriarchal conditions as an attempt to overcome the supremacy of the matriarchate. In addition, psychological research shows that homosexual men tend to have a family constellation characterized by an intrusive mother and an absent or rejecting father; that male homosexuals do not usually develop strong attachments to their fathers and that they report stronger identification with their mothers and weaker identification with their fathers; and that mothers of male homosexuals have been found to be closely bound with their sons and relatively uninvolved with their husbands.[16]

Despite such findings, in truth, no one knows whether homosexuality is a psychological problem due to faulty parenting or whether it is a natural human variation. Much of the confusion results from cultural prejudice, which leads researchers to fail to distinguish between causal relationship and correlation. Because two events occur in relationship to each other does not mean that one event causes the other. For instance, one can just as easily conclude from the above evidence that homosexuality is not caused by a weak father-son relationship, nor by a strong mother-son bond, but that homosexuality inherent in the son causes these kinds of relationships to develop. This conclusion is arrived at by reasoning that sons who are born homosexual are experienced as different by fathers who place a great stress on gender normality and who then withdraw from their sons and become rejecting. The son then turns to the mother for comfort and develops a stronger bond with the mother than with the father. Unlike psychological research that inculpates either father or mother or both in the genesis of homosexuality, current research on identical twins and on brain anatomy lends support to the idea that homosexuality is a biological variation, not a neurotic sexual problem.[17]

In contrast to homosexuality, homoerotic anxiety is clearly not a biological condition but an intense psychological conflict in which heterosexual men are obsessed with the fear that they will discover that they are actually homosexual. Yet the psychological theory used to explain homosexuality—the pattern of a weak, nonmasculine father combined with an overly intense and exclusive relationship between mother and son—is no more adequate in explaining homoerotic anxiety than it is explanatory of homosexuality.

Clinical material gathered from the analysis of a number of male patients who experienced intense homoerotic anxiety indicates that their anxiety is not an attempt to be more masculine through overcompensation. Rather, it results from the one-sided identification with a limited masculine viewpoint and consequent rejection of the feminine. These men were all raised in an environment where the females were essentially weak, dependent, nurturing servants to superior, dominating, physically powerful, tough men who lacked feeling, creativity, and spontaneity. The patients strongly identified with this limited image of the masculine. There was no question of inner femininity or contrasexuality. Rather than the normal, archetypal family relationship's being reversed, as Jungian theory argues it may be in the development of homosexuals, it was exaggerated.

Symptomatically, homoerotic anxiety intruded into the conscious lives of these individuals in an obsessive and compulsive manner. Typically, they found themselves compelled to look at the genital area of other men or they wondered how big their penis was compared to other men. For instance, one patient refused to join a health club for fear that he would not be able to avoid staring at other men's penises in the locker room.

All these men feared affection for other men as a sign of homosexuality and defended against their fears by paranoid thoughts of other men coming on to them. Quite naturally, such fear affects the transference relationship with male analysts.

For example, Sam, a twenty-five-year-old analysand, had an irrational fear of being attacked by strangers on the street. During one session he reacted with hostility to what I considered a series of helpful and correct interventions. When I pointed out his anger, Sam said he experienced my interpretations as hostilely motivated and refused to be affected by them. Subsequently, he dreamed of a black man stabbing him in the back. I suggested that he was afraid of being penetrated from the rear in an aggressive manner and that he experienced my interventions not as a helpful act but as a form of homosexual rape.

Reluctantly, Sam admitted that he had felt warm, grateful feelings for me after my previous interpretations. But he had been upset by my leaning forward as I made my comments. Both his feelings and my physical movement had been assimilated by his homoerotic complex. Sam understood his warm feelings as an erotic homosexual reaction. My leaning forward was distorted into an invitation to closer physical intimacy. His fantasy about the intention of my movement and his erotic response was then defended by angry feelings.

Sam's paranoid defenses kept him always on guard against my discovering his secrets. During one session he embarrassedly described a fantasy he had the previous evening when he heard the elevator door in the building of his residence open onto his floor. Sam had imagined that I was sneaking down the hallway in order to listen at his door and discover him doing something illegal. He, in turn, would quietly approach and open the door in order to catch me spying. When I commented that the theme of the fantasy was his being caught at some illicit activity, he immediately associated it to the discovery of homoerotic feelings.

Angry thoughts about women also aroused anxiety in these men that they were homosexual. They understood their devaluation of women as a general hatred of them, which they assumed indicated that they really wanted to be with a man. Sam, for instance, treated his previous female analyst with the disdain reserved for the depreciated women in his personal background. According to Sam, she became enraged by his demeaning behavior and attacked his masculinity, telling him that his behavior indicated that he was really defending against homosexual urges. Her retaliatory aggression terrified Sam and further aroused his homoerotic anxiety, not only because of her angry declaration about his feared homosexuality, but because his fear of her indicated to Sam that he was not as powerful with women as his dominant father and so must be homosexual.

I will try to explain the relationship that I have noticed between a rigid male gender role, a devalued femininity and symptoms of homoerotic anxiety.

Jung assumed that a primary motivation in the psyche is the instinctive drive for wholeness, the union of opposites. One manifestation of that drive is the impulse to unite masculine and feminine elements in the personality.[18] For a man, Jung believed, the symbolic goal of union can be concretely achieved only if those attributes that exist as unconscious potential in the anima can be developed into conscious attributes integrated by the ego. But how is that possible when what is associated with the feminine has been so devalued and rejected by a rigid and one-sided view of the masculine?

So far I have discussed the anima as a symbol of undeveloped potential in a man, as a repository for aspects of the total personality that a man is not allowed to recognize or develop because of the limitations of gender role. As an archetype, however, the anima is more than just a structure housing undeveloped contents; it is also a dynamism that is teleologically oriented—that is, the anima has an instinctive goal. Jung goes so far as to suggest recognizing the anima as an autonomous personality in her own right, with a will and intentionality of her own.[19]

If we assume that the anima's goal is to fulfill the psyche's drive toward wholeness, to be the other half of the totality symbolized as the union of masculine and feminine, then we would expect that those undeveloped qualities associated with the anima would be driven toward development, toward union with the masculine ego consciousness. Ideally, one would want this totality to be an intrapsychic phenomenon, an experience of inner union in which the masculine ego becomes aware of, embraces, and develops the qualities symbolized by the anima.

But if, because of the limitations imposed on the ego by a rigid gender identification, the anima's drive to achieve union is frustrated, it is possible that the anima might choose to satisfy its need for masculine connection elsewhere. The anima might try to connect with the necessary masculine characteristics that will complete the drive toward wholeness by an attraction to another man.

Since constellated complexes and archetypes are accompanied by particular body and feeling sensations, the individual would experience a physical as well as an emotional and psychological attraction. While the psychologically naive individual would perceive only the phenomenon of male-male interaction, the mediated psychological dynamic would be between inner feminine and outer masculine, and the true psychological dynamic would be a teleological drive for conscious awareness of the totality symbolized as masculine and feminine.

Let me illustrate with an example. During his third year of therapy Sam had a dream in which a young semideveloped female figure, whom Sam had earlier in the dream rejected, became interested in another man. Sam awoke filled with anxieties about homosexuality.

During his therapy session Sam said the other man in the dream was a friend toward whom Sam had noticed erotic feelings. Sam said this man was effeminate, which turned out to mean he was vulnerable and open with his feelings and had a respectful relationship with his girlfriend. Sam then engaged the female dream figure in an active imagination. Rather than rejecting her as he had in the dream, he accepted her into a relationship and they had a dialogue. In brief, she told Sam that they both needed to grow and could only do so in a relationship. If Sam refused to relate to her, then she would find another man to take his place, but she had to develop.

As Sam sat quietly reflecting on this exchange, he realized that the attraction toward his friend was not his but hers. Sam merely identified with the affective and body sensations that took place in the common physical and psychological home that he and the anima shared.

Sam then had a kind of fantasy vision during which he experienced a swirling mass of energy that he knew was the essence of femininity. This energy filled him with such an empty cavernous ache that he despaired of ever filling it. It was a part of his essential being. Another swirl of energy then flowed directly into the first, filling it completely and perfectly. Sam knew that it was the essence of masculinity. Then came the intuitive realization that the driving force behind his homoerotic fears was the need for the feminine to be filled and completed by the masculine, a need that was being ignored by a one-sided identification with a limited and rigid masculine viewpoint that depreciated and rejected the feminine from his totality.

This numinous experience was a projection of what Jung called the divine syzygy, the tendency for masculine and feminine images to occur together.[20] It was very healing and led to Sam's concerted and successful effort to change his attitude toward the value of the feminine both in his interpersonal relationships and with the inner feminine. Step by step with the relaxing of his rigid gender identity and the differentiation and integration of the anima, Sam experienced a diminution of his homoerotic anxiety.

CONCLUSIONS

From a Jungian point of view, psychopathology is viewed symbolically as well as symptomatically. Symbols provide direction to a person's development; they function as small signposts in a larger process of directional change. A symbol misunderstood, a developmental direction not followed, will often appear as a symptom that grips the person and forces his attention. The urge to submit, for instance, is often misunderstood as indicative of sexual perversion because of the value placed in our society on "masculine" assertion, logic, and willpower. Such a symptom can be very frightening to the individual who experiences himself as dominated by compulsions toward activities considered perverse.

When a man resists the need to submit to the transformative process, the urge to submit may appear as a neurotic symptom. As a symptom, submission is a perversion in which one person gives himself over completely to the domination of another. If the symptom is looked at symbolically, however, the Godlike qualities attributed to the dominant person by the submissive can be understood as a symbolic expression of the individual's need for psychological and religious meaning. Through submission a person can recognize that life is lived for the sake of something greater and more important than the ego and its perceptions. The ego becomes servant to that greater thing. This something may be called by many different names, depending on one's personal spiritual orientation and temperament. One may submit to the whole personality, the Self, or God. When misunderstood, this religious urge is lived out symptomatically; unconsciously, the individual seeking religious experience through complete surrender to God or the Self surrenders instead to the domination of sadists.

To redeem the anima, an experience unconsciously urged by the teleological drive inherent in the psyche, a man needs to recognize, develop, and integrate into his conscious personality the characteristics symbolized by the anima. Doing so has the effect of transforming the ego identified with the collective and familial values of the persona and affords the individual an opportunity to approach the experience of wholeness—never achieving it, since that is not our lot as human beings, but approximating it.

As in any redemptive process, a price must be paid. The price for a man is the experience of inadequacy and shame that initially accompanies the violation of internalized collective values. The fear of death and the experience of depression are two other aspects of the suffering attendant upon the transformative experience.

Redeeming the anima results in the transformation of the man. Integrating the previously rejected qualities leads to an experience of disorganization and reorganization, symbolized by images and experiences akin to death and rebirth. A broadening of the personality results. The man's conception of himself enlarges into that of a male human being, and he is released from his identification with the gender role aspect of the persona, the shell of collective identification and adaptation.

Epilogue

This book has been about a process of masculine transformation motivated by a teleological urge inherent to the psyche. The process of transformation leads men into and through a one-sided identification with the masculine gender role toward a condition of wholeness, a condition I call being a male human being.

What in ourselves and our society hinders or aids this process? How can we consciously raise sons who are capable of experiencing a secure masculinity and who can ultimately submit to the transformation of their masculine gender role?

A too-early emphasis on androgyny done at the behest of political correctness is harmful to masculine development. It is important for boys to first master the traditional masculine gender role of our culture—the instrumental/active dimension. Competence in this role provides a basis of security that allows for future development. Failure at this early task leads to defensive masculinity, a masculinity always looking for security through exaggeration of the traditional characteristics. The boy cannot transform what he does not securely have.

The father is a critical factor in the attitude the son takes toward his masculinity. The son wants to identify with a strong, capable, valued father. A relationship of warmth and affection is essential for this identification to be healthy. The son needs to see his attempts to emulate his father accepted and praised; he needs his father to agree that he is similar to the father and for the father to be proud of that similarity.

This implies to the son not only the father's pride in himself as a man, but also that the son is able to acquire a valuable masculinity through identification.

In a similar way it is important for the mother to value her husband and his embodiment of traditional masculinity in front of her son. She, too, needs to accept that the boy wants to be like his father, not like her. Mothers who are insecure and feel rejected by the boy's need to emulate the father can undermine a necessary process in the son's masculine development. If the mother denigrates her husband in front of the son, the son will view the father as powerless, without value, and the identification will not fill the boy with pride in himself. After all, what is the value of being like someone you do not admire?

While it is important to learn to appreciate the values and traditions of the collective in which we are raised, it is equally important to raise sons capable of standing against the collective. It is only those men who have the psychological strength that comes from confidence in their masculinity and value as human beings who will have the ability to consciously suffer separation from collective containment and approval and develop their masculinity beyond the traditional.

To raise sons who can develop beyond the traditional masculinity and have the courage to ultimately explore the other side of human potential, the value of women and the traditional feminine characteristics—the expressive/passive dimension—must be emphasized from the beginning. Even at the height of the conformist stage, when the son emphasizes the value of the masculine over the feminine characteristics, it is important that the father not participate in the denigration of the feminine. Denigration of the feminine characteristics by the father, or his humiliation and domination of the mother, results in an alienation of the boy from half of his human potential. A capable mother who manifests both the expressive/passive as well as the instrumental/active characteristics is essential, as well as a father who is respectful of the mother and the traditional feminine characteristics.

If the son grows up with respect for the traditional feminine characteristics, he will not fear that part of his personality when the teleological urge presents them during the phase of development when the tension and reconciliation of opposites becomes paramount. Rather, he will turn to that part of his human potential with the awe and pleasure that is its rightful due.

Notes

CHAPTER 1: THE BASIC SPLIT

1. See "To Predict Divorce, Ask 125 Questions," *New York Times*, August 11, 1992. Also see the following (full references for all works cited in the notes may be found in the bibliography): E. E. Maccoby, "Sex Differences in Intellectual Functioning"; M. D. Gall, "The Relationship between Masculinity-Femininity and Manifest Anxiety," pp. 294–95; T. C. Hartford, C. H. Willis, and H. L. Deabler, "Personality Correlates of Masculinity-Femininity," pp. 881–84; P. H. Mussen, "Some Antecedents and Consequents of Masculine Sex-typing in Adolescent Boys," p. 506; P. H. Mussen, "Long-Term Consequents of Masculinity of Interest in Adolescence," pp. 435–40.

2. J. Harrison, "Warning: The Male Role May Be Dangerous to Your Health," pp. 65–86; C. A. Nathanson, "Illness and the Feminine Role: A Theoretical Review," pp. 57–62; "Long Ignored, Prostate Cancer Gets Spotlight as Major Threat," *New York Times*, November 13, 1991; "Stereotypes of the Sexes Persisting in Therapy," *New York Times*, April 10, 1990.

3. S. L. Bem and E. Lenny, "Sex Typing and the Avoidance of Cross-Sex Behavior," pp. 48–54.

4. J. H. Block, "Conceptions of Sex Role: Some Cross-Cultural and Longitudinal Perspectives," pp. 512–26; J. T. Spence, R. Helmreich, and J. Stapp, "Ratings of Self and Peers on Sex-Role Attributes and Their Relation to Self-Esteem and Conceptions of Masculinity and Femininity," pp. 29–39; S. L. Bem, "Sex-Role Adaptability: One Consequence of Psychological Androgyny," pp. 634–43.

5. L. Kohlberg, "A Cognitive-Developmental Analysis of Children's Sex-Role Concepts and Attitudes," pp. 82–173.

6. J. Loevinger, "The Meaning and Measurement of Ego Development," pp. 195–206.

7. Block, "Conceptions of Sex Role."

8. C. G. Jung, CW 14, par. 671.

9. Other theorists have also taken the view that inherent in the human psyche are structures that cause information to be organized in ways that are typically human. In the field of psycholinguistics, for instance, Chomsky developed the viewpoint that the ability to acquire language

is an innate characteristic of humans as a species. He suggests that the innate predisposition of the child to learn language does not predispose the child to learn any specific language. The competency is content free in that it is the ability to learn any grammar, not a particular one. When the "deep-seated formal universals" are presented with a body of spoken language, the person develops the syntactic and semantic structures that correspond to the presented language. Once these structures are developed, the child can generate and understand new sentences that it has never heard before (N. Chomsky, *Aspects of the Theory of Syntax*).

Similarly, other psychologists besides Jung speculate that the acquisition of gender roles may also be due to innate structures. Pleck, for example, suggests that an apparatus for learning gender roles similar to Chomsky's language-learning apparatus may act as a processor of gender role images and linkages that are visible to the child. He argues that the brain may have an area that is predisposed toward categorizing in terms of gender. Such a hypothesis suggests that gender and all its trappings have the same kind of evolutionary history as does language, and that the brain has developed specialized dispositions toward gender categories just as it seems to have developed a unique capacity to cope with language. Thus there may be an inherent readiness to attend to stimuli related to gender, a readiness that produces the acquisition of gender roles. Such a position does not imply that ideas about gender are immutable. As language usage not only among individuals but also among cultures evolves over time, so are gender role attitudes, beliefs, and behaviors modifiable, both for the individual and for the society (J. Pleck, "Masculinity-Femininity: Current and Alternative Paradigms," pp. 161–78).

10. C. G. Jung, cw 9i, par. 155.

11. C. G. Jung, cw 18, par. 1228.

12. C. G. Jung, cw 13, par. 476.

13. M. Mead, *Male and Female*, pp. 114–15.

14. C. G. Jung, cw 13, par. 220.

15. C. G. Jung, cw 14, par. 671.

16. One danger in assuming the existence of innate masculine and feminine principles is that the principles are often not examined to see whether they actually reflect current or historical cultural prejudices. Unexamined, the principles inevitably become concretized and are used to "explain" normative differences between the genders that may really be no more than sociocultural biases. Instead of realizing that the principles themselves may be the result of an internalization of social norms, the external situation is simply assumed to be a projection of an innate

psychological condition. Norms become reified into "principles." A normative psychology based on innate factors results.

Psychologists establish norms by asking a large number of men and women to say which items on a list are indicative of masculinity and which are characteristic of femininity. Items that are generally answered one way by males and another way by females are used to construct a test of masculinity-femininity. People who subsequently take such tests are then compared with the norms and determined to be either more or less representative of the masculine or feminine gender roles. For instance, men who are highly masculine in a traditional way rate themselves as decisive and capable of making hard decisions divorced from concerns for the feelings of others. Women who are highly feminine rate themselves as sensitive to feelings and relationships.

Depth analysts often use mythology to create norms in a similar way. In mythology, a simple dichotomy often prevails between male sky/sun and female earth/moon deities. Characteristics associated with the mythological male and female deities are assumed to represent projections of underlying masculine and feminine principles and form a kind of normative test.

The problem with the mythological test is similar to the psychological test: both do no more than distinguish sociocultural attitudes. Neither can answer the question of whether men are more active and instrumentally oriented than women due to an underlying masculine principle, or whether the degree of activity and instrumentality is a function of how education and social expectations for men and women differ culturally and historically. Neither can say whether the male norms of activity and instrumentality are innate or merely a compensatory reaction to another underlying reaction—the expressive dimension, for instance, which is considered feminine.

17. There is evidence to support this idea. One study examined the behavior of four-person groups of high school students consisting of two males and two females who were unacquainted and who were matched as to race, social class, and degree of experience in teaching or verbal ability and cognitive style. The study also included all-male and all-female groups, similarly matched. The task of all the groups was to play a decision-making game that required them to agree on a series of paths by which to move a token from one side of a game board to another (M. Lockheed and K. Hall, "Conceptualizing Sex as a Status Characteristic: Applications to Leadership Training Strategies," pp. 111–24). Results supported the common norm that men are more instrumental and active than women and emerge as leaders in groups composed of males and females. In fact, men were seven times as likely as females to emerge as leaders in groups composed of males and females.

But were the results due to the men being inherently more instrumental and active than women, or were they due to the women's tendency to identify with a social norm that says that in the presence of men they should be less active and instrumental? This question was answered when the all-male groups were compared to the all-female groups. There were no differences between the mean number of acts initiated by the females and by the males. Females were just as active and instrumentally oriented when with other females as men were with other men or as men were with females.

Perhaps the true innate difference, then, lies in men and women together; that is, there might be an innate difference that causes men to be more active and dominant with females and the latter to be submissive to men when the two genders are together. Such reasoning is representative of the traditionalist view that males are naturally more dominant than females and that females should accept their more submissive role vis-à-vis men.

The study also speaks to this question. Females were given the opportunity to develop instrumental experience and competence in an all-female group, then placed in a mixed group of males and females. Results showed that engaging in the task first with other females significantly increased the number of instrumental acts initiated by females in mixed-sex groups; that is, experience that bred competence was the factor decisive in how active and task oriented a female was.

From this we can conclude that females and males do not differ in any innate way, either in terms of activity levels, overall task orientation, or leadership abilities. There are no differences between all-male and all-female groups in these respects nor in mixed groups when the females were given experience in these areas. The traditionalist idea that men are more instrumental and active than women owing to some innate differences, in aggression or anything else, is refuted by these experiments. Women are as capable of task-oriented instrumental behavior, activity, and leadership as men.

The position I take differs from the traditionalist idea that the observed differences between men and women are due to innate differences and from the strict social-learning hypothesis that attributes all differences to internalized norms. Rather, I am suggesting that there is an archetypal tendency to split psychic reality into opposing dimensions and that one primary set of oppositional categories is the instrumental/active and expressive/passive. The tendency toward such differentiation, I believe, depends basically on the human psyche's proclivity to differentiate all situations into opposites. Because of the child's need to develop an appropriate gender role distinct from the opposite sex, and because of social pressures that cause the initial gender role to be rigidly conformed to, men have become identified with the instrumental/active dimension and women with the expressive/passive.

Since these categories are based on archetypal dynamics, not innate gender differences, we could predict that both dimensions would occur and organize a situation even if only one gender were present. This expectation is borne out in a series of studies of all-male groups that found the same differentiation into instrumental and expressive roles as occurs in mixed-gender groups such as families and those designed to solve tasks (R. Bales and P. Slater, "Role Differentiation in Small Decision-Making Groups").

CHAPTER 2: MALE-MALE COMPETITION

1. See C. Allen's three reviews of the relevant literature: "Studies on sex differences," pp. 294–304; "Recent studies in sex differences," pp. 394–407; and "Recent research on sex differences," pp. 342–54.

2. R. Bly, *Iron John;* J. S. Bolen, *Gods in Everyman.*

3. Males are generally considered to be more aggressive than females. The difference is often attributed to the hormone testosterone, which in adults exists on the average of ten times more in men than women. High testosterone levels have long been known to typify the dominant males in groups of primates, such as baboons, and in unusual groups of men such as prison inmates and hospitalized psychiatric patients. The same high testosterone levels have been found in men who seek social dominance in normal realms of life. The relationship between testosterone and aggression is emphasized by research that shows that if testosterone is administered to females they too become aggressive and dominant. Male-hormone treatment of pregnant primates, for instance, increased the incidence of rough-and-tumble play among their female offspring; in humans, girls whose mothers were treated with male hormones while they were pregnant were later more vigorously active and more tomboyish than other girls (J. Money and A. A. Ehrhardt, "Prenatal Hormonal Exposure: Possible Effects on Behavior in Man").

Concluding that males are more aggressive than females due to the influence of testosterone leaves out the confounding effects of other hormones, however. For instance, the precursor hormone androstenedione has been implicated in the development of the extreme aggression characteristic of female hyenas ("Hyenas' Hormone Flow Puts Females in Charge," *New York Times,* September 1, 1992). Since human females possess significant levels of androsteredione, judging solely on the basis of hormones women may actually be as aggressive and competitive as men.

What is typically left out of the hormone discussion is the effect of the sociocultural environment, which interacts with and influences the expression of hormones. Family and society tend to reinforce aggressive traits in males and not in females. Our society, for instance, provides numerous blatant role prescriptions of aggressiveness for males, the most obvious being combat service in the military, the different toys that boys and girls are given to play with, and the extremely violent male heroes often found in novels, on TV, and in films. In contrast, our culture reinforces females in nurturance, dependence, obedience, and home-centered activities and discourages aggression that would be tolerated in males.

Thus, while hormones may be involved in producing aggression in both males and females, how and whether that aggression will be expressed is largely affected by personal and cultural history. Parents can interact with a boy in a way that will inhibit his aggression or with a girl in a way that will enhance hers.

The foregoing presentation has really been too simplistic because aggression and environment have not been adequately differentiated. Whether people are more or less aggressive is not dependent solely on hormones or whether their sociocultural environment encourages or discourages aggression. Further questions must be asked. What has aroused the aggression? How is the aggression being expressed?

Let's take the latter question first. Men are thought to be more prone to the physical expression of aggression than women. The population of prisons is often used as proof of that fact. Is the assumption correct and, if so, are males prone to physical aggression due to an inherent factor or to social conditioning? The answer depends on who is being compared. For instance, social class is a factor that determines whether aggression is expressed physically. Males from ghetto environments and working-class backgrounds express themselves through physical aggression more than males from higher socioeconomic backgrounds, perhaps because the latter have other, more constructive channels through which to express their aggression. As a matter of fact, females from ghetto environments, where physical violence is the norm, are also more prone to physical aggression than men from higher socioeconomic environments. Whether men are more expressive of physical aggression than women thus depends not only on possible innate factors but on such variables as social class.

So even though men have more testosterone and testosterone is related to physical aggression, and even though men generally express more physical aggression than women, whether the expression of physical aggression is a characteristic inherent to the masculine gender role is questionable.

4. J. Money, "Introduction," in *Men in Transition*, pp. 1–4.

5. C. G. Jung, cw 16, par. 434.

6. "In Fish, Social Status Goes Right to the Brain," *New York Times*, November 12, 1991.

7. "Aggression in Men: Hormone Levels Are a Key," *New York Times*, July 17, 1990.

8. T. Vanggaard, *Phallos: A Symbol and Its History in the Male World*, p. 120.

9. N. K. Sandars, trans., *The Epic of Gilgamesh*, p. 69.

CHAPTER 3: THE MAN AND THE MASK

1. C. G. Jung, cw 7, par. 246. In dealing with the formation of the gender aspect of the persona, Jung vacillated between the significance accorded to sociocultural effects and that accorded to innate masculine and feminine traits. Jung divided much of human potential into the opposites of Logos and Eros, equated Logos with the Chinese concept of yang and Eros with yin, and assigned Logos to the archetypal idea of the masculine and Eros to the feminine. Unfortunately, rather than remaining as genderless archetypal concepts, Logos and Eros rapidly became confused with the male and female gender, even in Jung's writings. For example, at times Jung wrote of Eros as if it were an expression of the "true nature" of women and that women's feelings were "always" directed toward the personal. Logic, objectivity, and an orientation toward the impersonal became characteristic of the true nature of men:

I use Eros and Logos merely as conceptual aids to describe the fact that woman's consciousness is characterized more by the connective quality of Eros than by the discrimination and cognition associated with Logos. In men, Eros, the function of relationship, is usually less developed than Logos. In women, on the other hand, Eros is an expression of their true nature, while their Logos is often only a regrettable accident. It gives rise to misunderstandings and annoying interpretations in the family circle and among friends. This is because it consists of opinions instead of reflections, and by opinions I mean *a priori* assumptions that lay claim to absolute truth. (Jung, cw 9ii, par. 29)

The difference in the orientation of their consciousness results in "natural" differences in the interests of males and females. This helps to explain why, according to Jung, men and women have become involved in different fields of experience. Logos leads men to be more interested in objective fields such as science and technology. Eros leads women to be disinterested in such topics:

But, just as a woman is often clearly conscious of things which a man is still groping for in the dark, so there are naturally fields of experience in a man which, for woman, are still wrapped in the shadows of non-differentiation, chiefly things in which she has little interest. Personal relations are as a rule more important and interesting to her than objective facts and their interconnections. The wide fields of commerce, politics, technology, and science, the whole realm of the applied masculine mind, she relegates to the penumbra of consciousness; while, on the other hand, she develops a minute consciousness of personal relationships, the infinite nuances of which usually escape the man entirely. (Jung, cw 7, par. 330)

At other times, Jung wrote as if he believed that the consciousness of men and women were determined not by innate factors but by the cultural milieu. For example: "A woman possessed by the animus is always in danger of losing her femininity, her adapted feminine persona, just as a man in like circumstances runs the risk of effeminacy" (Jung, cw 7, par. 337). In equating masculinity and femininity with an adapted persona, Jung implies that the masculine and feminine roles are formed in relationship to the sociocultural environment.

Not only is what one is defined by culture, but also what one is not: "The fact is, rather, that very masculine men have—carefully guarded and hidden—a very soft emotional life, often incorrectly described as 'feminine.' A man counts it a virtue to repress his feminine traits as much as possible, just as a woman, at least until recently, considered it unbecoming to be 'mannish.' The repression of feminine traits and inclinations naturally causes these contrasexual demands to accumulate in the unconscious" (Jung, cw 7, par. 297).

Jung's use of the term *repression* is instructive. In repression, an effort is made to keep a content dissociated from the ego consciousness so that the person does not recognize that content as part of his or her totality. But what is repressed could, without the expenditure of the repressive energy, just as well belong to the conscious personality. What is repressed is what is not acceptable to the ego consciousness.

It can be concluded that there exists an archetypal structure that mediates the relationship between the individual and the sociocultural environment. The persona, innate to the psyche, represents the readiness and ability for a human being to develop roles in order to adapt to and function in a particular social and cultural context. In addition, there exists an archetypal tendency for a man to seek to develop a masculine gender role as part of his persona and for a woman to seek to develop a feminine gender role as part of her persona. The particulars of those roles are determined by the sociocultural environment in which the individual is raised.

2. See, for instance, D. J. Levinson, C. N. Darrow, E. B. Klein, et al., *The Seasons of a Man's Life*; D. S. David and R. Brannon, "The Male Sex Role:

Our Culture's Blueprint of Manhood and What It's Done for Us Lately," pp. 1–45.

3. See W. Mischel, "A Social-Learning View of Sex Differences in Behavior," pp. 56–81.

4. R. E. Hartley, "Sex-Role Pressures and the Socialization of the Male Child," pp. 456–68.

5. J. S. Coleman, *The Adolescent Society*; B. Miller, "Lower-Class Culture as a Generation Milieu of Gang Delinquency," pp. 5–19; U. Hannerz, *Soulside*.

6. J. Balswick and C. Peek, "The Inexpressive Male: A Tragedy of American Society," pp. 363–68.

7. C. G. Jung, cw 6, pars. 738–40.

8. A. Katcher, "The Child's Differential Perception of Parental Attributes," pp. 131–43.

9. J. Kagan, "The Child's Perception of the Parent," pp. 257–58; W. Emmerich, "Family Role Concepts of Children Ages Six to Ten," pp. 609–24.

10. R. R. Sears, I. Rau, and R. Alpert, *Identification and Child Rearing*; P. Mussen and L. Distler, "Masculinity, Identification, and Father-Son Relationships," pp. 350–56.

11. S. Freud, *New Introductory Lectures*, p. 118.

12. J. Money and A. Ehrhardt, *Man and Woman, Boy and Girl*.

CHAPTER 4: MY FATHER, MY SELF

1. M. E. Lamb, "Father-Infant and Mother-Infant Interaction in the First Year of Life," pp. 167–81.

2. M. Kotelchuck, "The Nature of the Child's Tie to His Father."

3. E. M. Hetherington, M. Cox, and R. Cox, "Family Interaction and the Social, Emotional, and Cognitive Development of Children following Divorce."

4. See W. C. Bronson, "Dimensions of Ego and Infantile Identification," pp. 532–45; P. S. Sears, "Child-Rearing Factors Related to Playing of Sex-typed Roles," p. 431; E. M. Hetherington, "A Developmental Study of the Effects of Sex of the Dominant Parent on Sex-Role Preference, Identification, and Imitation in Children," pp. 188–94; A. Bandura and R. H. Walters, *Adolescent Aggression: A Study of the Influence of Child-Rearing Practices and Family Interrelationships*.

5. U. Bronfenbrenner, "The Study of Identification through Interpersonal Perception."

6. D. B. Lynn and W. L. Sawrey, "The Effects of Father-Absence of Norwegian Boys and Girls," pp. 258–62.

7. H. B. Biller, *Paternal Deprivation.*

8. O. Kernberg, *Borderline Conditions and Pathological Narcissism,* pp. 275–79; H. Kohut, *Restoration of the Self,* pp. 98–101.

9. C. G. Jung, CW, 9i, par. 135.

10. See W. Steinberg, *Circle of Care: Clinical Issues in Jungian Therapy,* pp. 72–88.

11. See N. Chodorow, *The Reproduction of Mothering: Family Structure and Feminine Personality.*

12. C. G. Jung, CW 12, par. 99.

13. E. Abelin, "The Role of the Father in Core Gender Identity and in Psychosexual Differentiation."

14. E. M. Hetherington, "Effects of Paternal Absence on Sex-typed Behaviors in Negro and White Preadolescent Males," pp. 87–91.

CHAPTER 5: MASCULINITY AND ACHIEVEMENT CONFLICTS

1. N. T. Feather and J. G. Simon, "Reactions to Male and Female Success and Failure in Sex-linked Occupations: Impressions of Personality, Causal Attributions, and Perceived Likelihood of Different Consequences," pp. 20–31.

2. J. Nichols, "Causal Attributions and Other Achievement-Related Cognitions: Effects of Task, Outcome, Attainment Value, and Sex," pp. 379–89.

3. R. Levine, H. Reis, E. Sue, and G. Turner, "Fear of Failure in Males: A More Salient Factor than Fear of Success in Females," pp. 389–98.

4. Feather and Simon, "Reactions to Male and Female Success."

5. R. Bly, *Iron John.*

6. N. K. Sanders, trans., *The Epic of Gilgamesh,* p. 62.

7. Ibid., p. 63.

CHAPTER 6: POWER AND THE MALE GENDER ROLE

1. A. Adler, *Understanding Human Nature,* pp. 69–91.

2. I. K. Broverman, D. M. Broverman, F. E. Clarkson, P. S. Rosenkrantz, and S. R. Vogel, "Sex-Role Stereotypes and Clinical Judgments of Mental Health," pp. 1–7; L. Kohlberg, "A Cognitive-Developmental Analysis of Children's Sex-Role Concepts and Attitudes," pp. 82–173; M. Komarovsky, *Dilemmas of Masculinity: A Study of College Youth.*

3. F. L. Strodtbeck and R. D. Mann, "Sex-Role Differentiation in Jury Deliberations," pp. 3–11; F. L. Strodtbeck, R. M. James, and C. Haw-

kins, "Social Status in Jury Deliberations," pp. 713–19; J. O. Whittaker, "Sex Differences and Susceptibility to Interpersonal Persuasion," pp. 91–92.

4. P. Rosenkrantz, S. R. Vogel, H. Bee, I. K. Broverman, and D. M. Broverman, "Sex-Role Stereotypes and Self-Concepts in College Students," pp. 287–95; H. N. Mischel, "Sex Bias in the Evaluation of Professional Achievements," pp. 157–66; J. P. McKee and A. C. Sheriffs, "The Differential Evaluation of Males and Females," pp. 356–71.

5. Adler, *Understanding Human Nature,* pp. 132–33.

6. Kohlberg, "A Cognitive-Developmental Analysis."

7. N. Chodorow, *The Reproduction of Mothering: Psychoanalysis and the Sociology of Gender.*

8. E. Person, "The Omni-Available Woman and Lesbian Sex: Two Fantasy Themes and Their Relationship to the Male Developmental Experience," pp. 71–94.

9. E. M. Hetherington, M. Cox, and R. Cox, "Family Interaction and the Social, Emotional, and Cognitive Development of Children following Divorce."

10. Chodorow, *The Reproduction of Mothering.*

CHAPTER 7: SUBMISSION AND MASCULINE TRANSFORMATION

1. M. Eliade, *Rites and Symbols of Initiation,* pp. 25–28.

2. T. Vanggaard, *Phallos: A Symbol and Its History in the Male World,* pp. 59–70.

3. Ibid., pp. 23–49.

4. Eliade, *Rites and Symbols,* pp. 25–26.

5. J. V. L. Goodall, *In the Shadow of Man,* p. 227.

6. Vanggaard, *Phallos,* pp. 76–81.

7. C. G. Jung, cw 9i, par. 58.

8. C. G. Jung, cw 9ii, par. 29.

9. C. G. Jung, cw 7, pars. 300–301.

10. C. G. Jung, cw 6, par. 804.

11. C. G. Jung, cw 12, pars. 80–81.

12. C. G. Jung, cw 7, par. 339.

13. C. G. Jung, cw 12, pars. 192–93.

14. C. G. Jung, cw 7, par. 305.

15. C. G. Jung, cw 9i, par. 146.

16. N. L. Thompson, D. M. Schwartz, B. R. McCandless, and D. A. Edwards, "Parent-Child Relationships and Sexual Identity in Male and

Female Homosexuals and Heterosexuals," pp. 120–27; J. Chang and J. Block, "A Study of Identification in Male Homosexuals," pp. 307–10; J. Nash and T. Hayes, "The Parental Relationships of Male Homosexuals: Some Theoretical Issues and a Pilot Study," pp. 35–43; R. B. Evans, "Childhood Parental Relationships of Homosexual Men," pp. 129–35.

17. "Gay Men in Twin Study." *New York Times*, December 17, 1991; "Is Homosexuality Biological?" *Science*, August 30, 1991, pp. 956–57.

18. C. G. Jung, cw 16.

19. C. G. Jung, cw 7, pars. 296–340.

20. C. G. Jung, cw 9, II, pars. 20–42.

Bibliography

Abelin, E. "The Role of the Father in Core Gender Identity and in Psychosexual Differentiation." Read at annual meeting of the American Psychoanalytic Association, Quebec, 1977.

Adler, A. *Understanding Human Nature.* New York: Greenberg, 1927.

Allen, C. "Studies on Sex Differences." *Psychological Bulletin* 24 (1927).

————. "Recent Studies in Sex Differences." *Psychological Bulletin* 27 (1930).

————. "Recent Research on Sex Differences." *Psychological Bulletin,* 32 (1935).

Bales, R., and P. Slater. "Role Differentiation in Small Decision-Making Groups." In *Family, Socialization, and Interaction Process,* edited by T. Parsons and R. F. Bales. Glencoe, Ill.: Free Press, 1955.

Bandura, A., and R. H. Walters. *Adolescent Aggression: A Study of the Influence of Child-Rearing Practices and Family Interrelationships.* New York: Ronald Press, 1959.

Barry, H., M. K. Bacon, and I. L. Child. "A Cross-Cultural Survey of Some Sex Differences in Socialization." *Journal of Abnormal and Social Psychology* 55 (1957).

Barry, W. A. "Marriage Research and Conflict: An Integrative Review." *Psychological Bulletin* 73 (1970).

Bem, S. L. "Sex-Role Adaptability: One Consequence of Psychological Androgyny." *Journal of Personality and Social Psychology* 31 (1975).

Bem, S. L., and E. Lenny. "Sex Typing and the Avoidance of Cross-Sex Behavior." *Journal of Personality and Social Psychology* 33 (1976).

Bem, S., W. Martyna, and C. Watson. "Sex Typing and Androgyny: Further Explorations of the Expressive Domain." *Journal of Personality and Social Psychology* (1976).

Biller, H. B. *Paternal Deprivation,* Lexington, Mass.: Heath, 1974.

Block, J. H. *The Child-Rearing Practices Report.* Berkeley: Institute of Human Development, University of California, Berkeley, 1965. (Mimeo)

————. "Conceptions of Sex Role: Some Cross-Cultural and Longitudinal Perspectives." *American Psychologist* (1973).

Bly, R. *Iron John: A Book about Men.* Reading, Mass.: Addison-Wesley, 1990.

Bolen, J. S. *Gods in Everyman.* San Francisco: Harper and Row, 1989.

Bronfenbrenner, U. "The Study of Identification through Interpersonal Perception." In *Person Perception and Interpersonal Behavior*, edited by R. Tagiuri and L. Petrullo. Stanford, Calif.: Stanford University Press, 1958.

Bronson, W. C. "Dimensions of Ego and Infantile Identification." *Journal of Personality* 27 (1959).

Broverman, I. K., D. M. Broverman, F. E. Clarkson, P. S. Rosenkrantz, and S. R. Vogel. "Sex-Role Stereotypes and Clinical Judgments of Mental Health." *Journal of Consulting and Clinical Psychology* 34 (1970).

Cano, L., S. Solomon, and D. Holmes. "Fear of Success: The Influence of Sex, Sex-Role Identity, and Components of Masculinity." *Sex-Roles* 10, nos. 5–6 (1984).

Chang, J., and J. Block. "A Study of Identification in Male Homosexuals." *Journal of Consulting Psychology* 24 (1960).

Chodorow, N. *The Reproduction of Mothering: Psychoanalysis and the Sociology of Gender.* Berkeley and Los Angeles: University of California Press, 1978.

Chomsky, N. *Aspects of the Theory of Syntax.* Cambridge, Mass.: MIT Press, 1965.

Coleman, J. S. *The Adolescent Society.* New York: Free Press, 1962.

David, D. S., and R. Brannon. "The Male Sex Role: Our Culture's Blueprint of Manhood and What It's Done for Us Lately." In *The Forty-Nine Percent Majority: The Male Sex Role*, edited by D. S. David and R. Brannon. Reading, Mass.: Addison-Wesley, 1976.

Eliade, M. *Rites and Symbols of Initiation.* New York: Harper and Row, 1958.

Ellis, L. J., and P. M. Bentler. "Traditional Sex-determined Role Standards and Sex Stereotypes." *Journal of Personality and Social Psychology* 25, no. 1 (1973).

Emmerich, W. "Family Role Concepts of Children Ages Six to Ten." *Child Development* 32 (1961).

Evans, R. B. "Childhood Parental Relationships of Homosexual Men." *Journal of Consulting and Clinical Psychology* 33 (1969).

Feather, N. T., and J. G. Simon. "Reactions to Male and Female Success and Failure in Sex-linked Occupations: Impressions of Personality, Causal Attributions, and Perceived Likelihood of Different Consequences." *Journal of Personality and Social Psychology* 31, no. 1 (1975).

Feldman-Summers, S., and S. B. Kiesler. "Those Who Are Number Two Try Harder: The Effects of Sex on Attributions of Causality." *Journal of Personality and Social Psychology* 30 (1974).

Fenichel, O. *The Psychoanalytic Theory of Neurosis.* New York: Norton. 1945.

Freud, S. *New Introductory Lectures.* Translated by J. Strachey. New York: Norton, 1965.

———. "Some Character Types Met With in Psycho-analytic Work: Those Wrecked by Success" (1916). In *Standard Edition of the Complete Psychological Works,* edited by James Strachey. vol. 14. London: Hogarth Press, 1981.

Gaeddert, W. P., A. Kahn, R. L. Frevert, and R. Shirley. "Role Model Choice: Who Do Women Say Their Models Are?" Paper presented at the meeting of the Midwestern Psychological Association, April 1981.

Gall, M. D. "The Relationship between Masculinity-Femininity and Manifest Anxiety." *Journal of Clinical Psychology* 25 (1969).

Goodall, J. V. L. *In the Shadow of Man.* Boston: Houghton Mifflin, 1971.

Hannerz, U. *Soulside.* New York: Columbia University Press, 1969.

Harrison, J. "Warning: The Male Role May Be Dangerous to Your Health." *Journal of Social Issues* 34 (1978).

Hartford, T. C., C. H. Willis, and H. L. Deabler. "Personality Correlates of Masculinity-Femininity." *Psychological Reports* 21 (1967).

Hartley, R. E. "Sex-Role Pressures and the Socialization of the Male Child." *Psychological Reports* 5 (1959).

Hetherington, E. M. "A Developmental Study of the Effects of Sex of the Dominant Parent on Sex-Role Preference, Identification, and Imitation in Children." *Journal of Personality and Social Psychology* 2 (1965).

————. "Effects of Paternal Absence on Sex-typed Behaviors in Negro and White Preadolescent Males." *Journal of Personality and Social Psychology* 4, no. 1 (1966).

Hetherington, E. M., M. Cox, and R. Cox. "Family Interaction and the Social, Emotional, and Cognitive Development of Children following Divorce." Paper presented at the Johnson and Johnson Conference on the Family, Washington, D.C., May 1978.

Horner, M. "Toward an Understanding of Achievement-Related Conflicts in Women." *Journal of Social Issues* 28, no. 2 (1972).

Johnson, P. "Women and Power: Toward a Theory of Effectiveness." *Journal of Social Issues* 32, no. 3 (1976).

Jung, C. G. *Collected Works*. 20 vols. Translated by R. F. C. Hull. Edited by H. Read, M. Fordham, G. Adler, and W. McGuire. Princeton, N.J.: Princeton University Press, 1953–79.

Kagan, J. "The Child's Perception of the Parent." *Journal of Abnormal and Social Psychology* 53 (1956).

Kahn, A. "Reactions of Profeminist and Antifeminist Men to an Expert Woman." *Sex Roles* 7–8 (1981).

Katcher, A. "The Child's Differential Perception of Parental Attributes." *Journal of Genetic Psychology* 87 (1955).

Kernberg, O. *Borderline Conditions and Pathological Narcissim*. New York: Aronson, 1975.

Kipnis, D. *The Powerholders*. Chicago: University of Chicago Press, 1976.

Kohlberg, L. "A Cognitive-Developmental Analysis of Children's Sex-Role Concepts and Attitudes." In *The Development of Sex Differences*, edited by E. Maccoby. Stanford, Calif.: Stanford University Press, 1966.

Kohut, H. *Restoration of the Self*. New York: International University Press, 1977.

Komarovsky, M. *Dilemmas of Masculinity: A Study of College Youth*. New York: Norton, 1976.

Kotelchuck, M. "The Nature of the Child's Tie to His Father." Doctoral dissertation, Harvard University, 1972.

Lamb, M. E. "Effects of Stress and Cohort on Mother- and Father-Infant Interaction." *Developmental Psychology* 12 (1976).

———. "Father-Infant and Mother-Infant Interaction in the First Year of Life." *Child Development* 48 (1977).

Lederer, W. *The Fear of Woman.* New York: Harcourt Brace Jovanovich/Harvest, 1967.

Levine, R., H. Reis, E. Sue, and G. Turner. "Fear of Failure in Males: A More Salient Factor than Fear of Success in Females." *Sex Roles* 2, no. 4 (1976).

Levinson, D. J., C. N. Darrow, E. B. Klein, et al. *The Seasons of a Man's Life.* New York: Knopf, 1978.

Lockheed, M., and K. Hall. "Conceptualizing Sex as a Status Characteristic: Applications to Leadership Training Strategies." *Journal of Social Issues* 32 (1976).

Loevinger, J. "The Meaning and Measurement of Ego Development." *American Psychologist* 21 (1966).

Lynn, D. B., and W. L. Sawrey. "The Effects of Father-Absence on Norwegian Boys and Girls." *Journal of Abnormal and Social Psychology* 59 (1959).

Maccoby, E. E. "Sex Differences in Intellectual Functioning." In *The Development of Sex Differences,* edited by E. E. Maccoby. Stanford, Calif.: Stanford University Press, 1966.

Mahler, M., F. Pine, and A. Bergman. *The Psychological Birth of the Human Infant.* New York: Basic Books, 1976.

McKee, J. P., and A. C. Sheriffs. "The Differential Evaluation of Males and Females." *Journal of Personality* 25 (1957).

Mead, M. *Sex and Temperament in Three Primitive Societies.* New York: Morrow, 1935.

———. *Male and Female: A Study of the Sexes in a Changing World.* New York: Dell, 1949.

Miller, B. "Lower-Class Culture as a Generation Milieu of Gang Delinquency." *Journal of Social Issues* 14 (1958).

Miller, D. R., and G. E. Swanson. *The Changing American Parent.* New York: Wiley, 1958.

Mischel, H. N. "Sex Bias in the Evaluation of Professional Achievements." *Journal of Educational Psychology* (1974).

Mischel, W. "A Social-Learning View of Sex Differences in Behavior." In *The Development of Sex Differences*, edited by E. E. Maccoby. Stanford, Calif.: Stanford University Press, 1966.

Money, J. "Introduction." In *Men in Transition*, edited by K. Solomon and N. Levy. New York: Plenum Press, 1982.

Money, J., and A. A. Ehrhardt. "Prenatal Hormonal Exposure: Possible Effects on Behavior in Man." In *Endocrinology and Human Behavior*, edited by R. P. Michael. London: Oxford University Press, 1968.

———. *Man and Woman, Boy and Girl*. Baltimore: Johns Hopkins University Press, 1972.

Mussen, P. H. "Some Antecedents and Consequents of Masculine Sex-Typing in Adolescent Boys." *Psychological Monographs* 75 (1961).

———. "Long-Term Consequents of Masculinity of Interest in Adolescence." *Journal of Consulting Psychology* 26 (1962).

Mussen, P. H., and L. Distler. "Masculinity, Identification, and Father-Son Relationships." *Journal of Abnormal and Social Psychology* 59 (1959).

Mussen, P. H., and E. Rutherford. "Parent-Child Relations and Parental Personality in Relation to Young Children's Sex-Role Preferences." *Child Development* 34 (1963).

Nash, J., and T. Hayes. "The Parental Relationships of Male Homosexuals: Some Theoretical Issues and a Pilot Study." *Australian Journal of Psychology* 17 (1965).

Nathanson, C. A. "Illness and the Feminine Role: A Theoretical Review." *Social Science and Medicine* 9 (1975).

Neumann, E. *The Origins and History of Consciousness*. Princeton, N.J.: Princeton University Press, 1971.

Nichols, J. "Causal Attributions and Other Achievement-Related Cognitions: Effects of Task, Outcome, Attainment Value, and Sex." *Journal of Personality and Social Psychology* 31 (1975).

Parsons, T., and R. F. Bales. *Family, Socialization, and Interaction Process*. Glencoe, Ill.: Free Press, 1955.

Person, E. "The Omni-Available Woman and Lesbian Sex: Two Fantasy Themes and Their Relationship to the Male Developmental Experience." In *The Psychology of Men*, edited by G. I. Fogel, F. M. Lane, and R. S. Liebert. New York: Basic Books, 1986.

Pleck, J. "Masculinity-Femininity: Current and Alternative Paradigms." *Sex Roles* 1 (1975).

Raven, B. H. "Social Influence and Power." In *Current Studies in Social Psychology*, edited by I. D. Steiner and M. Fishbein. New York: Holt, 1965.

Rosenkrantz, P., S. R. Vogel, H. Bee, I. K. Broverman, and D. M. Broverman. "Sex-Role Stereotypes and Self-Concepts in College Students." *Journal of Consulting and Clinical Psychology* 32 (1968).

Sanders, N. K., trans. *The Epic of Gilgamesh*. London: Penguin Books, 1960.

Sears, P. S. "Child-Rearing Factors Related to Playing of Sex-typed Roles." *American Psychologist* 8 (1953).

Sears, R. R., I. Rau, and R. Alpert. *Identification and Child Rearing*. Stanford, Calif.: Stanford University Press, 1965.

Spence, J. T., R. Helmreich, and J. Stapp. "Ratings on Self and Peers on Sex-Role Attributes and Their Relation to Self-Esteem and Conceptions of Masculinity and Femininity." *Journal of Personality and Social Psychology* 32, no. 1 (1975).

Steinberg, W. *Circle of Care: Clinical Issues in Jungian Therapy*. Toronto: Inner City Books, 1990.

Strodtbeck, F. L., and R. D. Mann. "Sex-Role Differentiation in Jury Deliberations." *Sociometry* 19 (1956).

Strodtbeck, F. L., R. M. James, and C. Hawkins. "Social Status in Jury Deliberations." *American Sociological Review* 22 (1957).

Thompson, N. L., D. M. Schwartz, B. R. McCandless, and D. A. Edwards. "Parent-Child Relationships and Sexual Identity in Male and Female Homosexuals and Heterosexuals." *Journal of Consulting and Clinical Psychology* 41 (1973).

Toby, J. "Violence and the Masculine Mystique: Some Qualitative Data." *Annals* 36, no. 4 (1966).

Vanggaard, T. *Phallos: A Symbol and Its History in the Male World*. New York: International Universities Press, 1972.

Whittaker, J. O. "Sex Differences and Susceptibility to Interpersonal Persuasion." *Journal of Social Psychology* 66 (1965).

Index

C. G. Jung Foundation Books

*Published in association with Daimon Verlag, Einsiedeln, Switzerland.